Y0-ARM-039

# AMERICA'S
# TENNIS BOOK

**Books by Curtis W. Casewit—**

The Skier's Handbook
Ski Racing: Advice by the Experts
The Mountaineering Handbook
The Hiking-Climbing Handbook
America's Tennis Book
and other titles

# AMERICA'S TENNIS BOOK

Curtis W. Casewit

CHARLES SCRIBNER'S SONS · NEW YORK

Copyright © 1975 Curtis W. Casewit

Library of Congress Cataloging in Publication Data

Casewit, Curtis W
   America's tennis book.

   Bibliography: p.
   1. Tennis. 2. Tennis—United States. I. Title.
GV995.C23        796.34'2'0973        74–10714
ISBN 0–684–13900–6

This book published simultaneously in the
United States of America and in Canada -
Copyright under the Berne Convention

All rights reserved. No part of this book
may be reproduced in any form without the
permission of Charles Scribner's Sons.

1 3 5 7 9 11 13 15 17 19 C/MD 20 18 16 14 12 10 8 6 4 2

Printed in the United States of America

# Contents

Part Six—The Passionate Tennis Player

# Author's Foreword

How does a writer choose his subject? Sometimes his subject chooses him. Ever since my youth, for instance, I felt deeply drawn to the mountains; so it was logical to write books about rock climbing and hiking, skiing and ski racing. I had already played some tennis when I suddenly faced a personal crisis, which was intensified by distressing family problems. I began to play tennis every day and fell in love with this sport. Tennis meant escape from the self; on a court, one could banish worry and overcome anxieties. All at once, the problems seemed simpler, and gradually, there came solutions. Tennis helped me to better health as it helps thousands of other people.

Here was the subject then! I *had* to write a book about tennis. But what kind of book? I decided that I had to assemble most of the current tennis information; the facts would have to be selected with an eye on timelessness and long life. As I began my research, I discovered that certain tennis subjects had never been tackled, or not tackled in depth. My focus therefore would be on some little-known aspects of the sport. I found, for example, that no how-to manual dealt with the important topic of tennis resorts, tennis hotels, tennis "ranches," or tennis clinics. It wouldn't have been hard to obtain information on tennis vacations by mail—to draw from public relations releases, as some travel guides do. I preferred to visit most of the tennis places myself, and describe briefly what I saw. Strangely, I could discover no books in the field that dealt with tennis etiquette or careers related to the sport, or most important, tennis books that illuminated the possible injuries. These were fresh subjects, then, which had to be backed by solid how-to-play descriptions and by some helpful chapters on competitive playing.

The balance of *America's Tennis Book* concentrates on answering the vital questions on technique, equipment, and strategy. Tennis had given me so much that I was prepared to repay in kind; I spent long hours corresponding with tennis professionals, tournament players, and physicians. I traveled the length and breadth of North America to interview the authorities, to watch them teach and see them in court action. So many people gave their time that one would need an extra chapter to name them all.

The book may have been impossible to write if had not been for the personal assistance from the following experts:

Roy Emerson, of the Laver-Emerson Tennis group, Lake Conroe, Houston, Texas.

Vic Braden and Fred Port, Braden Tennis Colleges, Lake Tahoe, Calif., and Recreation & Resort Enterprises, Los Angeles, California.

John Gardiner and his teaching staffs, Gardiner Tennis Ranches, Scottsdale, Arizona.

Gardnar Mulloy, Miami Beach, Florida (and Todd Harris, Orlando, Florida).

Don Kerbis, Kerbis Tennis Ranches, Watervliet, Michigan.

Cliff Buchholz, "The Timbers," Steamboat Springs, Colorado.

Bill Smith, the likable resident pro, Palm Springs, California.

Dr. R. P. Nirschl, Washington, D. C., and Dr. Arnold Heller, Denver, Colorado.

Chet Murphy, University of California in Berkeley, California.

My sincere thanks also go to Pro Charlene Grafton in Alabama; Joan Rosenthal, USLTA, New York; Helen Moak, Philadelphia; Gilbert Richards, Cincinnati, Ohio; and Forry Mulvane, Western Air Lines, Los Angeles. I was grateful for the long interviews granted by Arthur Ashe, Roscoe Tanner, Marty Riessen, Billie Jean King, Rosie Casals; and thanks to John Edwards, Enid Slack, and Mike Narracott, who introduced me to the champions. Lastly, I want to express my deep appreciation to Irwin Hoffman, Heather Ridge Racquet Club, Denver, who read and corrected the entire manuscript, and to my fellow Coloradans Rich Hillway, Ade Butler, Vernon Scott, Jim Landin, Stephanie De Fina Johnson, Loren Dunton, and Anne Dye, who made valuable suggestions.

May they play tennis forever!

C. W. C.

# PART ONE

## The Case for Tennis

*Photo by Bob McIntyre.*

# CHAPTER 1

# Who Plays Tennis?

The tennis call "Anyone for tennis?" has long become a robust chorus, "Everyone for tennis!" (well, almost). Statistically, there're three times as many American tennis players as skiers and nearly twice as many tennis players as golfers. Pick a city at random and let the officials impress you with sheer numbers: San Diego, California, for instance, operates some one hundred municipal courts, with many more to come; most of them see steady use from dawn until the artificial lights go off late at night. During the early seventies the megalopolis of Los Angeles contained about half a million players.

According to an A. C. Nielsen survey, America will have some sixteen million racket owners by the year 1980. The forecast is based on an annual growth rate, and the figure makes sense. No one can deny an ongoing tennis boom. Every year, for example, Americans spend over $500 million for tennis merchandise, boosting the profits of manufacturers, wholesalers, and retailers. All do a big business. During the past ten years, for instance, the sale of tennis balls has quadrupled. According to pollster L. Harris, tennis keeps gaining players and spectators at a faster rate than any other U.S. sport.

It is true that the American public seeks to make the most of its leisure time. In addition, thousands of Americans are fascinated by the huge sums paid to name competitors in various tournaments. A women's tennis circuit can attract more than $1 million in prize money. Male racket stars can earn from $250,000 to $350,000 a year; in addition, thousands of persons now make a living in other phases of the sport. (See special chapter on careers.) The explosion continues via clinics for instructors, "tennis scholarships" to develop players, travel funds for junior competitors, and free equipment for the best teen-agers.

The USLTA (U.S. Lawn Tennis Association) promotes the sport on all levels, especially through schools. It is true that many scholastic coaches favor baseball and football, and neglect tennis, especially in the Midwest. The USLTA is working on the problem. An official explains the position: "One important aim of physical education directors should be to interest more young people in playing rather than watching tennis. If boys and girls learn to love the game during their schooldays, they will continue long after graduation. During the war, tennis was one of the sports recommended by the Army Air Forces Technical Training Command, because "playing contributes greatly to endurance, speed, agility and coordination."

The national enthusiasm shows up in a hundred ways. A Midwestern executive heads for his city park at 6 A.M. and pounds balls for a full hour against a backboard. He does this from Monday to Friday all summer. An Ohio mother-to-be wrote to a magazine that she was four-months' pregnant; her doctor had agreed that she could continue her favorite recreation as long as she felt like it. The woman's worry was that she didn't want to get into "any awkward playing habits" created by her condition. Did the magazine's readers have any suggestions? A California club pro was not astonished: one of the club members was getting lessons until seven days before delivery, and returned to the courts again two weeks later. In New Mexico, a group of

Interest in tennis has increased considerably during the past decade. *Vail Photo by Peter Runyon.*

isolated high-altitude scientists became so engrossed with the game that they persuaded the U.S. Air Force to build a court for them. This was done at great expense on their remote 9,000-foot mountain outpost. Enthusiasm! A Chicago printer set out to design bumper stickers, decals, cocktail napkins, greeting cards, and arm patches with only two words: "Think Tennis."

The enterprise succeeded because more Americans *are* thinking tennis. The newcomers belong to all walks of life. Unlike rock climbing, skydiving, or ski racing, tennis takes no physical courage. Long-time pros assure us that anyone—men, women, and children—can learn to play, according to their own lights. Statistically, at least 30 percent of America's players are women, but we seem to have almost as many females as males on the courts. The sexes stand an equal chance when it comes to recreational tennis. On a tournament level, however, the muscular equipment allows men to run faster and to serve with greater force.

It is important to note that advanced age is no barrier to learning (or playing). The resident professionals of various resort hotels occasionally tell about eighty-year-old ladies who insist on taking lessons. The essentials have been taught to the obese, the lame, and the hopelessly out-of-condition. Vic Braden, the Dean of America's "tennis colleges," has held two-day clinics for wheelchair patients, the blind, for youngsters aged three, and for frankly unathletic people. Braden's philosophy is a positive one. "We can teach anyone who *wants* to learn. The right attitude is important. The higher the student's interest level, the greater the chance." Genuine desire is easy to recognize, of course, and positive thinking and motivation can work wonders for tennis.

Numerous case histories prove this theory. One pro claims that because of will power, a man with a false leg now plays fair tennis. A Florida coach prefers to turn back the pages of tennis history to 1938, when an ambitious young girl named Doris Hart first reported for a lesson. The coach watched the girl play and noticed her slight but distinct limp. Despite her permanent handicap she was intent on becoming a competitor. The coach eventually decided that she was a "natural." To be sure she would never be able to cover the court as rapidly and effectively as other people. The pro took movies of her game, and after a study, he concluded that a big serve and a strong volley would compensate for her weakness. Doris Hart worked hard, and it took her five years to develop into a first-class player. She was to become the national junior singles champion, then America's number-one woman player, and eventually won at the Wimbledon Center Court. She *wanted* to learn and she did.

Doris Hart had an uncommon athletic ability. The average adult novice can get along on much less. A minimum of coordination, a sense of balance, timing, good eyesight, and normal reflexes can suffice. Some previous experience in other games, such as basketball or baseball, are considered helpful.

Not all sports seem beneficial, though. To illustrate: a table-tennis champion must unlearn the tendency toward the extra-flexible wrist; the latter is generally kept rigid in tennis. Likewise, while years of soccer activity make for strong legs, the soccer player gets into the habit of moving up close to the ball, which is not the case in tennis. The player here keeps his distance, so that he can hit.

How about the person who always avoided athletics? A skillful teacher can impart the tennis strokes and stances to almost anyone. But you will enjoy your net time better—and become fatigued less quickly—if you're in fair physical shape. A get-and-stay-fit outlook is therefore important. Let us look at a man with a sedentary job, for instance. He may be thirty-year-old CPA who keeps books for a large hotel. After a few tennis lessons and some practice, he realizes that he gets out of breath too soon. Although he is in good health, his heart pumps too hard. He has leg cramps, followed by muscle pains. On the advice of his instructor, the CPA therefore makes a few simple resolutions:

1. He'll no longer use the hotel elevator. He'll walk up or down instead.
2. At home, he'll avoid driving his automobile for minor shopping. He'll refrain from drive-in banking, drive-in lunches, and other stay-seated temptations.
3. He'll go to the mail box on foot.
4. If he must cut his lawn, he'll prefer a hand mower to a power mower.

5.   He'll try to be physically active for at least forty minutes a day around his home. Gardening, walking, and even car-washing qualify as exercise.

Many instructors hold that regular tennis playing itself will increase running ability and stamina. The better condition will make us play better, too. Veteran physical educators, however, insist on some pre-tennis exercises and on supplementary workouts. These need not take long. Just five minutes of rope jumping can do wonders. We may compare some of the tennis footwork to that of boxing, and boxers favor rope jumping too. Five minutes should yield at least one hundred jumps, one foot at a time, then with both feet. Fast hiking helps those who live in or near the mountains. Mountain climbers who scale rock walls naturally do good things for their legs. But even the weekend walker, who handles fifteen to twenty miles, has achieved something for his or ? physique.

Cycling also prepares a person for the tennis court. Squash is a possibility. Instructors at the Timbers Tennis School in Colorado are convinced that yoga influences the average student's flexibility, vitality, and balance. Hatha Yoga is therefore part of this school's daily program. A special instructor also teaches Laya Yoga to sharpen concentration. How about golf? As a conditioner it may not be taxing enough, especially if the golfer patronizes electric carts. We improve our bodies in the swimming pools or the ocean only if we actually *swim* for thirty to fifty minutes. Most people apparently just loaf in the water.

Instructors agree that jogging and running have the greatest effect on fitness for tennis. The speed of jogging approximates fast walking, and it is good advice that you should ease into this program. As a newcomer, you might begin the first week's session this way:

Jog for one minute.
Walk for one minute.
Alternate between the two for five minutes, then rest five minutes, then repeat. The day's exercise time need not exceed ten minutes at first.

The first couple of weeks should involve mainly walking at different speeds interspersed with short periods of jogging and two or three periods for stretching and recovery. In later weeks, a recreational player can gradually increase his workouts. Instead of jogging he can run. "Alternately sprint hard for twenty-five steps and then jog for fifteen" suggest the instructors of the John Gardiner tennis ranches. Veteran tennis pros also recommend "wind sprints," jumping jacks, or running backward. Extra-eager athletes will lengthen their work periods, while other persons may want to drop jogging and running altogether and head for the tennis courts instead.

Some coaches believe in the merit of "shadow tennis" or simulated tennis, which requires no racket and familiarizes you with the motions. According to the coaches of the U.S. Lawn Tennis Association, the following exercises will lead to tennis skills:

1. Knee-bending (A crouch will be necessary for low balls.)
2. Lunging (essential to complete the stroke)
3. Back bending (needed for service form)
4. Skipping sideways (gliding or drifting into position)
5. Running backwards and forward (a tennis essential)
6. Squeezing a tennis ball and relaxing (You must have strong forearms.)

Certain isometrics can be recommended to those adults who get serious enough to dream of competition. Many coaches endorse the use of bar bells to strengthen us for tennis.

Our muscles have an amazing ability to grow through steady employment. Take the thousands of small, unused fibers. They multiply when we make a continuous demand on them. In addition, the tiny capillaries bring more oxygen and other nourishment to our muscles.

A better player learns to use the entire body and therefore needs less strength. That is why a slight young woman can sometimes outplay a male powerhouse. Her opponent may use his biceps wrongly while her own weight distribution, rhythm, and motions are perfect. A beginner still needs a minimum of muscle, however, and should have enough stamina to last through at least thirty or forty minutes of running on the court. Better recreational players ought to play six games (one set) without falling to pieces. Bear in mind that a minor tournament means playing two sets in succession. So much for the physical side.

How about mental equipment?

Tennis is based on the ability to concentrate. One must have the capacity to keep the eyes on the ball, even the hundreth ball within an hour. Total attention must be riveted to the trajectory of this round object as it crosses the net toward us. We must return it time and again. We must be able to "place" the ball and serve accurately as well. There is no time to look at other people or to admire the deep blue sky. Most adults are able to concentrate, especially if tennis fascinates them. But a child's attention span is still limited. One instructor puts it this way. "A youngster *can* concentrate for a little while. But then comes a moment when he'd rather watch the birds fly." In addition to getting bored, small youngsters still lack the strength to hold a racket, even a "training" (light) racket.

What is the ideal age to start? The champion Roscoe Tanner began when he was six. Resident pros in resort hotels accept youngsters at that age for their first "lessons." For many cities' programs and leagues, youngsters of eight and up are acceptable. Specialized tennis camps ask that parents do not enroll their offspring before the ninth or tenth birthday. Teachers welcome children because they're faster learners than adults. Young people don't have to cope with bad old habits. And they like to experiment. Small tots also display a talent for imitation, which makes them prospects for quick learning.

Most children display good coordination and a quick eye. An adult's muscular and eye reflexes will diminish after the age of forty and fifty. A middle-aged man may be fond of tennis but he will be less flexible and slower than a 21-year old, besides getting exhausted within a shorter period. But physicians agree that healthy males should continue to play, as long as they understand their own physical limits. This becomes crucial for the average nonathlete of fifty or more who gets into this sport for the first time, or plans to intensify his playing schedule.

Since the 1960s, senior tennis became increasingly important in North America. Better national health and a longer life span automatically create a

"Anyone for tennis?" Everyone for tennis! Or almost everyone, including small children. *Photo courtesy Vic Braden Tennis College.*

greater number of old players. It is significant that modern corporation presidents and chairmen of the board often prefer a midday hour of forehands and backhands to the four-martinis lunch. White-haired statesmen have learned that they have a better chance to weather a crisis by heading for a tennis court. Many aging Hollywood and Las Vegas entertainers own their own fenced rectangles, and an older writer, James Michener, is known to play regularly.

The game serves as a fine diversion for the retired, and at tournaments one notices a remarkable number of rugged types long past their sixtieth and even seventieth birthday. Many of these seniors display perfect form; they compensate for their age by correct technique and by anticipating the flight of a ball. To be sure, many of these competitors already played for one or more decades, and can thus draw on experience.

The veterans have devised a number of special survival rules. Here are the major ones:

1.  They will only play after getting a green light from their physicians. Tennis can be strenuous enough to aggravate cardiac problems for persons over fifty.

2.  They'll resign themselves to the fact that their eye reflexes cannot adjust fast enough to a hard-hit ball. They may therefore prefer staying in the back court instead of hugging the net, where the ball reaches its greatest speed.

3.  They will attempt to conserve their strength by moving at a slower pace, by avoiding unnecessary running, and by economizing on every physical level. They will strive for fluid and not jerky motions, and will refuse to dash after impossible balls.

4.  Unless they feel up to it, they'll refuse to compete against young men, or compete only on their own terms.

5.  They'll prefer doubles because a doubles game does not require the coverage of a large surface.

6.  They won't play in the broiling sun but during the early-morning hours. They protect their heads with white hats. They will prefer natural light to artificial light.

7.  They'll avoid court surfaces that are hard on their legs, or rackets that are hard on their arms.

8.  They'll refuse to consider themselves in the league of such stars as Pancho Segura, Pancho Gonzales, Bobby Riggs, Don Budge, or other senior champions.

9.  They'll never expend more energy than they have available. Unless they're extremely tough, they'll only play one or two hours per day. But they know full well that they must not give up this sport and they must keep in motion.

Few senior tennis players will quarrel with the Greek sage who told us, "The old age of an eagle is better than the youth of a sparrow."

CHAPTER 2

The route to good tennis playing requires many hours on the courts. *Photo by Markow Photography for Gardiner Tennis Ranches.*

# How to Become a Player

While anyone can acquire the tennis basics with enough determination and persistence, some beginners underestimate the game. It is more difficult than they anticipate. The ball and the opponent are in motion, and it takes experience to achieve playing consistency. If there is a shortcut, it must be through *regular instruction by a professional.* As we've already seen, an instructor can do more with the well-conditioned, athletic student, but the pro prides himself in helping anyone at almost any age. In some instances, progress may be slow; in fact, some people may never get beyond a certain stage. The capable instructor tries his best, of course; he adapts himself to the physique and foibles of his students.

Group lessons are adequate, but for those who can afford them, private lessons speed up the learning process. To be sure, a pro will have an easier time to teach a woman than her own husband. Only the most gifted persons can teach *themselves* the delicate interplay of feet, shoulders, and arms by copying other players. The self-taught often wind up with unsound strokes and incorrect weight shifts. Bad technique becomes ingrained.

It is best to let a competent instructor lay a solid foundation, and the cost in time or money need not be excessive. Lessons may last for only thirty, forty-five, or sixty minutes; pros recommend one or (preferably) two lessons per week, either in a group or alone. The smaller the class, the more personal attention, of course. Three sessions per week naturally let you advance at a faster pace.

A week in a tennis clinic or at a tennis resort school usually results in quick learning progress. *Photo courtesy Vic Braden Tennis College.*

Many beginners make one mistake, however. They rely on lessons alone, and avoid the courts at other times. Instruction should be backed by at least twice the amount of court practice, which can follow on the heels of the lesson. A tennis novice can be compared to the novice skier who spends the morning in class and then tries out his new knowledge on the slopes in the afternoon. Keep in mind that a beginner's—or intermediate's—tennis lessons shouldn't be too far apart; it is easy to forget what an instructor told us a month ago.

One can only acquire tennis skills by hitting hundreds—thousands!—of balls from every angle. Practice may take several forms. Here are the avenues open to a beginner:

1.  He can play against someone else. This gives the most pleasure, if the other person is slightly more advanced.

2.  In some locales and on some courts, it is possible to utilize an automatic ball machine. The gadget may be impersonal, but it provides plenty of practice.

3.  One can bounce balls against a backboard or practice wall. This may not be as much fun as rallying with a live human being. But practice walls are fast and patient. They never give up.

4.  One can buy a special nylon net or a "tennis trainer" from a sporting-goods store. Both devices are useful.

Professionals can teach some elementary ball control in six to ten lessons; if feasible, instruction should continue for one to two years, during which a keen player tries to eliminate his weak spots. After an initial clinic, many people fail to brush up on their technique and strategy, and thus remain on the same level. A resident pro in Puerto Rico summed up the situation: "My feeling is that 95 percent of the population plays tennis but only 5 percent can be called actual tennis players." Some experts hold that lessons and practice should take precedence over playing matches. But many intermediates find it enjoyable to challenge any person in sight. Competition actually gives a special impetus to each hour on the court, and even a victory against another intermediate brings a sense of accomplishment.

Schools, churches, recreation departments, clubs, and even banks now go in for summer programs at low cost. Some instruction is gratis. *Photo courtesy United Banks Photography.*

The road to good timing, good rhythm, and the return of hard balls is paved with long, hard hours on cement, clay, or synthetic surfaces. Some advanced maneuvers such as "overhead smashes," "drop shots," or "lobs" require additional months of trial and error. The late Bill Tilden, one of America's tennis greats, always claimed that it "takes a year or less to learn the fundamentals. But it takes five years to make a tournament player and ten years to make a champion."

Average mortals content themselves with some initial group lessons. Costs vary from as little as one dollar per hour in various city recreational programs to twenty-five dollars and up for big-name instructors. The U.S. East and large cities exact more money than the West or South for private instruction. High rents add to costs in New York City's indoor courts. When shopping for tennis lessons, you should also realize that extras—like video-tape machines, for instance—drive up prices.

The cheapest adult classes are available through city parks and recreation departments and other municipal agencies. Sometimes there may be as many as ten to twenty students per court, and the teachers may know little more than tennis rules. But the rates are affordable by almost everyone. Certain community centers, YMCAs, YWCAs, and apartment-house complexes offer inexpensive tennis instruction to adults. Some high schools consider the sport as part of athletics, and most universities sharpen the tennis skills of their students. The teacher-pupil ratio may vary from 1 to 15 to 1 to 30. But the price is right and the old days of the super-tough martinet-type coaches are over at universities.

As collegians turn into better players and move on to earn a good livelihood, they join an indoor or outdoor club. Outsiders are often allowed to take lessons. Clubs of all kinds are multiplying in our multiplying suburbs; new clusters of town houses are being built with tennis students and aficionados in mind.

Once a rarity, there now exist more than one thousand indoor courts. Some are open from 7 A.M. to 11 P.M., and come equipped with assembly-line instruction, ball machines, and artificially lighted practice courts. A research firm estimates that by 1980, North America will have 150,000 outdoor courts. Some of these are municipally owned and therefore free or nearly so. (By contrast, only few public courts exist in Europe.) In a few big American cities, a player must buy a permit for the summer. Hourly court rates go on the bill if you play at elegant resorts. If you want to use one of the air-conditioned indoor facilities of a famous hotel in Acapulco, your hourly court rate can go as high as sixteen dollars for the privilege.

Some American towns are eager to get citizens and visitors started and to improve everyone's game. A community-service director in California, for instance, boasts that his desert city is recognized as the "Tennis Capital of the World." You can take lessons at the obligatory courts of the hostelries and the big clubs, or the city courts, which are floodlit at night. There are also the private courts. A Palm Springs matron once put it this way: "Everyone here has a swimming pool, but the real status symbol is a private tennis court—with an automatic ball server for those who want to practice alone, plus a visiting or private instructor."

Many young couples see their first forehand demonstration while spending a weekend at a better hotel. Indeed, few first-rate resort hostelries would dare operate without some tennis courts and a resident pro. Instruction is available at large motor inns and hotels as far south as Texas, along the eastern seaboard, in Illinois and, of course, in the West. In fact, many Americans combine a vacation with learning to play. The programs at the best tennis resorts (see Chapter 15) are thoughtfully planned. The vacationer is kept busy with skillfully arranged group and private lessons, classroom lectures, fast-moving outdoor drills, motion pictures, and reading material, followed by competition. Instead of spreading instruction over months as one would at home, you take a five- to seven-day course. Likewise, much work can be packed into the two-day "crash-courses" at a "tennis college."

A vacation can easily be parlayed into learning to play (or to play better). *Photo by Stott Shot.*

Concentrated schooling will cram a great deal of information into students' heads. No one could possibly pick up the game overnight; some tips thus may be forgotten, only to emerge again suddenly and mysteriously six months later. The professionals console us that even the most talented must expect frustrating moments.

Tennis skills are not acquired gradually but in stages. John Gardiner, who invented the concept of "tennis ranches," explains the process. He says: "You will have good days and bad days and you will reach many plateaus in your tennis ability. At times it will seem you are making great progress; then all at once it may appear that your game has come to a standstill and you can't do anything right. Don't be discouraged. It happens to everyone."

A tennis ranch such as one run by Don Kerbis in the Great Lakes area is an excellent place to acquire or sharpen tennis skills. *Photo by Don Kerbis.*

It is always best to be in the hands of a first-rate professional instructor. He can dissect strokes with care. He can analyze foot work and point out the tiniest flaw in your service. He can correct all facets of tennis technique, and if his first suggestion doesn't work, a seasoned pro can couch it into fresh words. Moreover, superior tennis schools use teaching aids that are unique.

Unfortunately, the public's demand for instruction generally exceeds the supply of skilled teachers. America still has no unified tennis system, and some instructors are weak in diagnosing a student's mistakes. A famous Davis Cup star does not necessarily do well with beginners, and a few advanced beginners have been known to pose themselves as expert instructors (especially of young girls).

You generally can count on a reliable staff by enrolling in one of the week-long resort programs, or by investing in a tennis-ranch vacation. The pioneers in the field pick only experienced assistants. Country clubs, private clubs, and top resort hotels also maintain high standards. The customer usually fares well, too, in local commercial indoor and outdoor installations. If you know someone else who takes lessons on a certain court, ask if the classes can be recommended.

How can you tell if someone is qualified to help you?

One of the best answers comes from Cliff Buchholz' tennis camps. Students are given a questionnaire to rate the competence of each instructor. Here are the revealing details:

|  |  | BELOW |  |  |  |
|---|---|---|---|---|---|
|  | POOR | AVERAGE | AVERAGE | GOOD | EXCELLENT |
| 1. Enthusiasm |  |  |  |  |  |
| 2. Ability to evaluate strength & weakness |  |  |  |  |  |
| 3. Knowledge of tennis |  |  |  |  |  |
| 4. Teaching ability |  |  |  |  |  |
| 5. Ability to communicate |  |  |  |  |  |

A good teacher treats his student as an individual, and he *likes* people. He takes an interest in someone's physical condition or health problem, and he enjoys giving advice about equipment. If the customer comes for a week's "immersion," the instructor makes himself available off the court to answer questions.

Buchholz' program in the Rocky Mountains is fairly typical for what happens on a tennis vacation. Apart from court work and practice, students get the benefit of other available recreation. In Colorado, for example, your week's schedule is as follows:

MONDAY—FRIDAY

| | |
|---|---|
| 9:00 A.M. | Breakfast |
| 10:00 A.M. | Tennis instruction on the courts |
| 12:00 Noon | Lunch |
| 1:00 P.M. | Free time (horseback riding, swimming, hiking, reading, going to town, etc.) |
| 3:00 P.M. | Tennis instruction on the courts |
| 5:30 P.M. | Free time (open court time, any of the activities listed above plus visiting the cocktail lounge.) |
| 7:00 P.M. | Dinner (steak rides on some evenings) |
| | Friday afternoon is free time (no tennis instruction.) |

SATURDAY

Supervised competition—tournaments; other activities.

Many resorts also operate a separate summer tennis camp for children. Instruction here takes place at different hours from those of grown-ups, or during different months. The same pros are used. Young people naturally have more time for a tennis school; their clinic lasts from two to six weeks. Parents have the choice of several hundred tennis camps that take only children and young adults. Such summer camps thrive in almost every U.S. state and Canadian province. It is important for parents to realize that a three-week children's tennis clinic necessitates good equipment and a well-assorted wardrobe. One typical camp recommends the following:

|                    BOYS                     |                    GIRLS                     |
|---------------------------------------------|----------------------------------------------|
| Tennis racket                               | Tennis racket                                |
| 6 tennis shirts                             | 6 tennis dresses or                          |
| 6 tennis shorts                             |    6 shorts and 6 shirts      |
| 6 pairs white socks                         | 1 sweater and 1 jacket                       |
| 1 sweater and 1 jacket                      | 1 pair white tennis shoes                    |
| 1 pair white tennis shoes                   | 1 bathing suit                               |
| 1 bathing suit                              | 1 bathing cap (optional)                     |
| 1 tennis hat                                | 2 pairs pajamas                              |
| 2 pairs pajamas                             | 1 beach towel                                |
| 1 beach towel                               | 2 street dresses and shoes                   |
| 6 changes underwear                         |    (for church, banquet and other) |
| 4 pairs jeans and shirts                    | 4 pairs jeans, 4 shirts                      |
| 1 warmup suit (optional)                    | 6 changes underwear                          |
| 1 laundry bag                               | 1 warmup suit (optional)                     |
| 2 pairs slacks, street shoes (for           | 1 laundry bag                                |
|    church if desired and banquet) | Toilet articles                         |
| Toilet articles                             | Musical instrument, if any                   |
| Musical instruments, if any                 | Stationery and stamps, if desired            |
| Stationery and stamps, if desired           | $25 of pocket money                          |
| $25 of pocket money                         |                                              |

At some camps, additional gear is needed for scuba diving, horseback riding, and mountaineering. All inclusive rates are usually from $300 upward, which means that only a small percentage of American families can send their children to such places. Besides, the minimum camp age is usually eight or ten and parents are likely to introduce their youngest to the "game" themselves.

For a child under six, the word "game" assumes great importance. A public playground, a backyard, or a quiet sidewalk does fine for the initiation. Bring the lightest possible racket. It should be a junior model; if the child is too small, the father can saw off the handle. Tennis balls should be extra-light; either utilize the nonpressure kind or select some that are fairly well worn down.

Young players can learn the game at hundreds of specialized summer camps. *Idaho State Photo.*

Some parents manage to give their tots an immediate "feel" for tennis. At first, a pavement or a house wall will suffice. A little girl can be shown how to enjoy herself by just "trampolining" a ball on her (horizontal) racket. Many fathers and mothers possess the imagination and patience to handle their preschooler's first efforts or to do well with pre-teeners. Certain pros specialize in teaching youngsters.

Young people should never be pushed into instruction. Just as an un-
wanted piano lesson can become drudgery, forced sports lead nowhere either,
especially under the supervision of a disciplinarian. Child experts have devel-
oped a number of "tricks" that amuse youngsters and bring out their playful-
ness. "Just keep them smiling and laughing," says Todd Harris, a respected
Orlando, Florida, pro. For a starter, Harris lets his little ones balance balls on
their rackets, and then run back and forth to the net. Harris encourages his
small first-timers to hit *him* with one shot over the net. A parent can also play
catch with youngsters at a distance of about fifteen feet. This teaches coordination of hands and eyes.

A child's catching (and fifteen-foot throwing) ability shows whether he
is ready for tennis. One can soon toss easy balls, letting the youngster hit them
back with the racket. At any stage, instructors do not criticize or laugh about
their charges. The beginner's efforts always earn praise.

The tennis profession also discovered long ago that some kind of score-
keeping speeds up the learning process. An instructor (or parent) can count
balls successfully whacked against a wall, banged onto the sidewalk, or returned across the net. Some child specialists teach service by counting the
number of balls that land correctly. A Colorado pro next arranges "mixed
doubles" for his tiny boys and girls. The "competition" takes place on the
service line instead of on the base line; the small-fry's serves thus clear the net
without trouble. Which "team" will serve accurately the most times and win
two soft drinks?

Immediate "competition" is also the idea behind the free mass classes of
the "National Junior Tennis League." Since its birth during the late sixties,
the NJTL brought tennis to youngsters (ages eight–sixteen) in Harlem, New
York, Richmond, Virginia, Philadelphia, Pennsylvania, and many other inner
cities. This youth program now comprises hundreds of coast-to-coast teams in
many state capitals, and fifty thousand boys and girls profit nationally from the
league.

Recreation departments teach for free or at a nominal charge. Programs
exist in most cities from coast to coast. A characteristic one takes place periodically in Dallas, Texas, where thousands of youngsters are treated to lessons

on some 150 public courts by the Dallas Parks & Recreation Department. States such as California and Florida encourage public instruction during the entire year, and the children's programs are in great demand.

The child moves from the elementary to intermediate class and to advanced playing. The next step is becoming a junior tennis "expert," and before we know it, the young people become adult experts themselves.

# PART TWO

## The Beginner's Tennis Primer

Specialty shops do the perfect string job. *Photo courtesy Ski, Inc.*

# CHAPTER 3

# What Equipment to Buy

It is fortunate that tennis doesn't demand as much from your pocketbook as many other sports. A rank beginner can get along at first with inexpensive equipment bought at a discount or department store. Large sporting-goods retailers run bargain sales in late fall because they must make room for other merchandise or next-year's fashions. If you buy in larger cities (and not at resorts), you'll save money too, because stores are in competition with one another. This results in fair prices.

A specialty tennis shop is always smaller than general sporting-goods retailers. Some specialty shops, like those in warm climates, sell tennis equipment the year round; other stores switch to ski gear in winter.

Should you patronize a specialist? That depends. An advanced player derives an advantage from such a merchant because the inventory will consist of quality merchandise. The beginner will get better service from the specialist, who expects a standard profit from the sale. Specialty shops seldom cut prices. (Discounters do.) Tennis shops generally have more knowledgeable personnel, too, and they're more patient with the customer. (If the salesman seems hurried, a beginning player may want to take his business elsewhere.)

Tennis equipment is available in a wide price range. A quality racket and the most expensive tennis shoes are fine for those beginners who can afford the extra cost. Remember, too, that the high retail price of famous-brand names includes the hefty costs of national advertising. (The customer pays part of the bill.) A young person or a child—or a wife who plays just occasionally —may wish to consider unknown racket brands and plain white canvas shoes. Likewise, a novice weekend netter need not patronize a specialty shop; on a public court fancy apparel is unnecessary.

This spend-little-at-first philosophy applies especially to average families and to the less affluent, and to those first-timers who are not sure whether they'll continue playing. At some later time, when an enthusiast discovers an almost magnetic attraction to tennis, better gear can mean a better game. A top-notch racket also boosts the morale of the beginner competitor. The four-times-a-week type will select a more costly racket, quality balls, good tennis shoes, and appropriate attire. (The latter is dictated by the locale; you naturally dress better at a resort or a tennis club.) At this point, the small, specialized shop can provide excellent counsel. The owner usually plays tennis himself. He carries mainly superior goods, and will stand behind each sale. (Most name brands normally come with a year's guarantee for material and workmanship. If either lets you down, you receive a replacement.) You also can deal with a pro shop at a club, hotel, or resort. The merchandise quality will probably match the service but at a slightly higher price; and the pro shop's range of selection is not quite as wide; many such outlets close after the tennis season.

# RACKETS

A surprise awaits the prospective player if he or she visits a tennis outlet for the first time. In the same vein, tennis magazines can be startling to a tyro.

What a variety of rackets! What proliferation of manufacturers, materials, sizes, names, and prices! A talk with an instructor and some intelligent browsing should slice through the confusion.

First of all, you'll have to decide how much you want to spend. Some beginners start with an inexpensive wood racket. Study the frame for symmetry, cracks, or breaks. The strings should be consistent and feel hard to your touch. Tap another frame against the racket face and listen; a high-pitched sound indicates adequate stringing. Some "bargains" naturally have a short court life.

It is wise to buy cheaply for young children; they'll outgrow their equipment in record time. The average adult can get started on an expenditure of

*Right.* Controversial question: wood or metal racket? Both have advantages and disadvantages. This wood racket suits many players.

*Left.* Metal rackets have become popular. They are particularly good for people with tennis elbow or similar problems, and they are often used in doubles.

$25 to $35. After tasting the pleasures of tennis, some enthusiasts decide to invest from $40 to $70 in a first-rate racket.

A racket comes with a handle, throat, and head. The handle is covered with a layer of leather or plastic. Proper weight is important; too-light or too-heavy a racket makes a difference on the court. If your racket feels like a feather, it will probably twist in your hand while playing. Too much weight can cause delayed stroking, increased effort, easier tiring, and perhaps a painful "tennis elbow." Don't decide until you've held several rackets; the salesman won't object to your shadow motions. "Feel" will help with your choice. Better players will care about "balance" created by heavier heads or heavier handles.

The size of the handle is a matter of personal preference. Put your palm around the butt; see if it is comfortable. Too-small a grip means poor control after ball contact; the racket can even fly out of your grip during a game. Conversely, some men make the mistake of favoring husky grips and heavier rackets because these look more "masculine."

A knowledgeable sporting-goods salesman—or tennis pro—can help you with sizes. One manufacturer advises newcomers as follows:

| IF YOUR GLOVE SIZE IS: | YOUR SUGGESTED GRIP SIZE IS: | YOUR RACKET SHOULD BE: | WEIGHT (WITH STRINGS) |
|---|---|---|---|
| **MEN** | | | |
| Up to 8 | 4 3/8 | Medium | 13 1/2 oz. to 14 oz. |
| 8–8 1/2 | 4 1/2 | Medium | 13 1/2 oz. to 14 oz. |
| 8 1/2–9 | 4 5/8 | Medium | 13 1/2 oz. to 14 oz. |
| 9 1/2–10 | 4 3/4 | Heavy | Over 14 oz. |
| 10 and over | 4 7/8 to 5 | Heavy | Over 14 oz. |
| **WOMEN** | | | |
| Up to 6 | 4 3/8 | Light | Under 13 1/2 oz. |
| 6 1/2 | 4 1/2 | Light | Under 13 1/2 oz. |
| 7–7 1/2 | 4 5/8 | Light | Under 13 1/2 oz. |
| 7 1/2–8 | 4 3/4 | Medium | 13 1/2 oz. to 14 oz. |
| 8 and over | 4 7/8 | Medium | 13 1/2 oz. to 14 oz. |

Young people between the ages of twelve and fourteen can use 13-oz. rackets and small grips. For small fry it is best to buy special 11- to 12-oz. gear with short handles.

Most beginners' tennis rackets are sold prestrung. The material is usually nylon. First-timers or novices derive little advantage from animal gut, which costs from $15 to $20. While gut strings are more responsive to your playing, they're also more delicate than nylon. Even the best gut—lamb—will deteriorate in heat, rain, or general humidity. That's why you should never leave a gut-strung racket overnight in a car trunk. Cold and sunlight are equally bad for such natural products. Nylon is sturdier, and stands up better under rainy or sizzling conditions. But nylon has too little "snap-back" or liveliness, and competitors seldom play with nylon strings.

The stringing tension varies with the material and grade. It is wise to have the shop pull the string tight enough so that it can no longer stretch, leaving no mobility. (A 50- to 65-pound pressure should do the trick.) Too much tightness can create muscle and elbow problems, especially in older players.

If the strings wear out, restringing should be considered if your racket frame is sound enough to make it worthwhile. Speciality shops are best for this work.

For many years the great sports controversy revolved around the two major racket materials: wood or metal? The choice is the customer's. He may start out with a wooden racket and later go to metal. There are advantages and disadvantages to either material. Both lend themselves to flexible or rigid frames. However, it is important not to be misled by the well-paid super-champions who endorse these products (sometimes without using them!). A famous autograph looks good on the handle but means little to the average weekend player. The buyer should give little credence to fancy names like "The Smasher," "The Regent," "The Court Star," "The Power Bat," and many others.

Luckily, there are enough ethical merchants who refrain from selling novices heavy sixty-dollar metal rackets.

The most popular material is a high-tensile aluminum. A quality aluminum racket—for which you pay from thirty to seventy dollars—can later offer a psychological boost when you get into matches against friends.

In the case of more expensive rackets, aluminum offers the advantage of reliable quality control during the manufacturing process. (Unfortunately, there are few cheap-quality metal rackets.) Thanks to open throats, aluminum feels lighter than wood and is therefore easier on the nonathlete. Metal presents little chance of warping, and it stores well. On the other hand, inexpensive metal rackets can develop grommet problems and strings will break easily. More important, some metal rackets pack such a wallop that the ball is difficult to control. Players often overshoot; strongly muscled men may even fire over high fences. The usual complaint is that metal can have a "trampoline-like" or a "slingshot" effect.

Metal rackets were already used by French champions during the 1920s, although it took an American firm until 1967 to introduce the first commercial model. Wood used to be—and still is—traditional. To be sure, wood feels more "natural," provides more resiliency, and allows more responsive stroking. Better players will demand many laminations. These add strength and flexibility.

The building of a top-quality wood racket is surprisingly complex. The operation may require twenty-five different wood pieces of several varieties. One racket brand, for instance, features nine laminations of strips that make up the main frame and handle. The manufacturer uses ash, beech, birch, maple, and hickory, because these are all strong, tough, and fairly heavy. The throat of the frame consists of light mahogany or sycamore, both beautifully grained. The eight pieces for the handle are mahogany or a light Nigerian material called obeche.

Many of the pros and instructors consulted for this book admitted a preference for wood. Rod Laver, for instance, found metal rackets "too fast." He always achieved more control with wood. Some instructors claim that wood is better to learn on, and a preventive for possible elbow strain.

On the negative side, wood may crack or splinter and therefore have a short life span. If you play much, a racket may last one year or less. This drives up your equipment costs, of course. The staff at one tennis school celebrates the end of a six-month season with a dramatic bonfire of old rackets.

One could sum up the pros and cons of the two materials in the following manner:

| WOOD | | METAL | |
|---|---|---|---|
| POSITIVE | NEGATIVE | POSITIVE | NEGATIVE |
| More ball control | Warping, | Even | Trampoline effect |
| Better feel | splintering | craftsmanship | Overpower |
| Less chance for | Needs pampering | Longer-lasting | Grommet problems |
| "tennis elbow" | (racket press, | Stores better | Quality at higher |
| Holds strings | etc.) | More power | prices than wood |
| Used by more pros | | Better for | |
| Inexpensive rackets | | nonathletes | |
| available | | Lighter (less wind | |
| | | resistance) | |

A lifetime instructor at a Palm Springs, California, resort, the respected pro Bill Smith, sums up the matter as follows: "Beginners can use metal or wood with equal results."

Metal rackets can be stored without the benefit of a tennis press, which is necessary for wooden ones. A racket cover always seems a good idea. Press and cover cost less than five dollars.

## OTHER TENNIS NEEDS

A beginner can get the first feel of tennis with inexpensive balls. They'll wear out fast and may then be replaced by something better. As always, one pays more for brand names, and for quality, which includes pure wool covers and pure rubber cores.

Balls are manufactured for all types of court surfaces (read the label before buying), for various elevations (high-altitude balls), for many kinds of light conditions (use yellow balls under gray or darkening skies), and for various kinds of players. If you report for your first forehand and backhand lessons, the instructor will probably let you hit extra-light balls. Good players

use heavier ones. Competitors usually have plenty of strength, and know how
to use it.

Tennis balls normally come in hermetically sealed cans, so a newcomer
has little chance of estimating the age of the product. Is it still fresh? Will the
balls bounce? Some bold discount-store customers open the tins and make
sure with a personal test against the floor. One can also tell that balls are dead
*without* resorting to measures that might upset a store detective. Merely shake
the can; if the balls move slightly, they're still good (reason: as air gets in, the
inside pressure will prevent the balls from budging). A ball naturally wears
out faster on a hard surface, and tournament players receive new ones for
every match. Some expensive brands last for many weeks of recreational
after-hours playing; some brands may lose their outer fuzz fast, which makes
them bounce too high. If dropped from about the level of your neck, a ball
should bounce no higher than your waist. Throw away balls that offer no
resistance to your squeeze. They're dead.

One final point: good manners dictate that players bring their own supply
to the rally; no one makes friends by always using someone else's balls.

Quality tennis shoes cost almost as much as street shoes. This is not
astonishing, because leather is now used. This improves the performance and
assures durability. The investment of twenty to forty dollars for a first-rate pair
is worthwhile for people who practice often and much. The cushioned soles
of these higher-priced tennis shoes absorb some of the shock of every leap and
allow running on cement and asphalt without discomfort. Leather uppers feel
better and protect delicate feet. The personnel in speciality shops sees to it
that you're fitted well. Take a trial walk. Your shoes should be comfortable.
The soles should grab and grip, thanks to a serrated pattern. Ankle-length
basketball footwear does not work out on the courts, nor do some tractionless
slick-soled sneakers or moccasins. Tennis shoes must be white, irrespective of
the material.

Leather footwear is unnecessary for the person who plays only on occasion or for someone just starting out. All stores sell acceptable canvas tennis
shoes for ten to twenty dollars. Inexpensive sneakers suffice for limited rallying, especially on softer courts. If you practice every day, an extra pair is

"White is (still) right" in men's tennis fashions, where designs change comparatively little. *Photo courtesy Catalina.*

recommended. Competitors and instructors are big consumers; some of them use up a good brand in a few weeks.

Men's tennis shoes are worn with thick wool socks (some players prefer a second thinner pair against their skin). Women look better in special socklets, also called half-sox, that do not protrude beyond the edge of the shoe.

Tennis clothing changes very little from year to year for men. Many clubs accept pastel colors, but "white is (still) right," behind most nets. White happens to be cooler, more dignified, and less confusing than gaudy colors.

Tennis shorts and a tennis shirt are worn by men. Chose the sizes for comfort. Avoid too much looseness or tightness.

For the male who plays much, several pairs of shorts and several shirts are essential; while one garment is at the laundry, you still have something else to wear. A V-style pullover or a tennis jacket protects the match player before and after a few sets. Warm-up pants and jackets come in white, dark blue, and other colors; the purchase adds another twenty to fifty dollars to tennis costs but pays off in fewer muscle pains or colds.

Women are thought to be more fashion conscious, and their apparel goes through occasional design changes. White will remain proper for many years to come. The trim on tennis dresses and ladies' tennis shirts and skirts should be kept to a minimum. (Colored adornments distract the other person.) While pastels rarely offend women's tennis etiquette, too much color—termed "peacock alley"—disturbs some pros and club managers. Tennis skirts were shortened through the years, and the panties have become more frilly, a develop-

The popular tennis dress. Pastel colors have shown up in recent years in women's tennis fashions.

ment frowned upon in some circles. Good taste should guide one in this department.

Women's tennis outfits can be bought from twenty to eighty dollars, with thirty dollars being a good average. If a woman plays every day, she can use a larger wardrobe, of course.

All players need head protection. It could be a brimmed white hat that absorbs the suns rays and shields the face or a tennis visor that keeps the sun out of one's eyes. Some people favor a headband. It holds long hair in place. It can be white or many-hued, Indian-style. Men sometimes wear baseball-type caps. Fortunately for the sport, only the well-paid professionals need to look totally up-to-date (which includes brightly colored shirts for male world championship players). Professionals and wealthy people are the customers for tennis gadgets such as $35 equipment bags, $25 racket covers, or a private restringing machine costing $500.

# CHAPTER 4

The correct grip improves your game. *Photo courtesy "Virginia Slims."*

# Tennis Grips, Stances, and Strokes

## GRIPS AND STANCES

Playing tennis starts with holding a racket correctly. For beginners, the so-called "Eastern" grip is best; it allows hitting forehands, which make up most of a game.

The grip is simple enough.

Set the racket face on its thin rim. The racket handle should point toward you.

Hold on to the racket face with your left hand. Let your right one stretch out parallel against the grip. Now shake hands with the racket butt. The thumb and fingers are wrapped comfortably around the handle, with the knuckles draped over the handle's wide side. Your forefinger and thumb should reveal a "V" along the thin edge of the handle.

Instructors have devised simple ways of teaching the forehand grip in starter classes. X's are painted on the hand and on the handle as shown. The hitter then has only to match the X's to place his hand on the racket properly. *Photo by Bob McIntyre.*

A slight (½-inch) adjustment of the "V" to the left (meaning that you'll have to turn the racket one notch to the right) produces the proper grip for the backhand.

The Eastern grip also allows basic serves. There are other grips, such as the "Continental" or the "Western," that interest more advanced players; beginners would only be confused at this point.

You'll easily understand the soundness of the "Eastern" hand and handle combinations by swinging the racket through the air. The proper grip will mean that your racket strings have a better contact with and control of the ball. Whether you hit a forehand or backhand, instructors consider accurate racket holding so important that at tennis clinics even *advanced* players must first demonstrate their grips.

Your grasp becomes slightly more firm as you hit a ball, but otherwise, there is no need for extreme tightness or extra looseness. (In the latter case, the racket may soar out of your hand.)

Technically accurate tennis also starts with a good waiting or "ready" position. The latter does not vary from beginner to top competitor; indeed, one can observe the identical stance on television during a professional big-money match.

The ready position is a classic one. Stand at the baseline, facing the net. Using an Eastern grip, point the racket toward your opponent's court. (The left hand steadies the racket throat.)

This novice demonstrates a ready position; it will eventually get even better, with the knees bent more. *Photo courtesy Vic Braden Tennis College.*

Your legs are comfortably apart. The body is somewhat forward, with the weight favoring the balls of your feet. The knees are slightly bent. Be as alert and ready as a 100-meter sprinter. Keep your eyes on the ball as it leaves the other person's racket.

You'll find it easy to comprehend the logic of the ready stance. It enables the player to start off in any direction. By first facing the net, one can storm forward or skip sideways; it is possible to pivot quickly toward a ball coming to the forehand side or to turn the shoulders to the left and retrieve a backhand ball.

In either case, it is important to understand one fundamental of tennis: you must always seek a steady platform before striking a ball. This is why experts use small, skipping steps as they head for the ball. Racket back, the players come to a standstill on a "platform" and *then* hit. Beginners often make the mistake not only running of toward their objective, but of *striking* on the run. As a consequence, the ball goes out. One instructor puts it this way:

> It has always been splendid advice to hurry, hurry, hurry into position so as to have more time for the actual stroking. Don't reverse this procedure—as many often do—by moving into position slowly and then have to hurry, hurry, hurry the execution of the stroke itself.

The "platform" can be compared to that of a skier, who also requires a "base" to achieve a turn.

# THE FOREHAND

Instructors often say that 60 to 70 percent of a tennis game consists of forehands, meaning that the ball is struck from the right side of the body. The forehand, therefore, will be taught first. Most people learn this stroke quickly enough. Because the ball is hit after a bounce on the ground, the forehand is called a "ground stroke."

Some tennis schools have built up almost foolproof methods to explain the mechanics. The student immediately understands that this basic stroke can be achieved only by *a sideways position to the net.* The swing requires preparation for the oncoming ball, good footwork and balance, and a steady wrist. The novice learns that the racket-holding arm must be back and ready long before the ball arrives. At the moment of impact, although slightly bent backward, the wrist is kept rigid. A flopping wrist can change the direction of a ball by as much as thirty feet.

The new player is also made to realize that a forehand involves not just the wrist, elbow, and arm, *but the entire body.* The shoulder does most of the work. Ideally, the motions are fluid and synchronized. Throughout, the arms only guide the ball; the rest is done by shifting your weight.

Here is the forehand, as taught in the United States. Follow it, step by step:

1.   Stand in the ready position, trunk to the net until you see the ball coming toward your forehand. As the ball approaches, turn to the right until facing the right sideline.

2.   At same time, step toward the ball with your left foot, pointing it diagonally toward your right sideline. The left foot is forward and about twelve inches ahead of right foot. The weight is on the left foot, knees bent slightly.

3.   Before the ball bounces, draw your racket back for the backswing, shifting the weight slightly from the left to the right foot. The racket should be back and perpendicular to the net. The arm should be fully extended, the wrist laid slightly back, but held firmly. Some instructors make you bring the racket back in a straight line; many schools teach a slightly upward backswing that can later swing forward in a loop.

4.   Watch the ball carefully. Make sure that you're not too close to it. This may require some short steps *away* from the ball. The beginner can handle a high bounce with greater ease by moving backward instead of forward. (Better players do the reverse, and catch balls on the rise.) The lower the ball, the more kneebend, and the lower your swing.

5.   Hit the ball evenly in front of you before it reaches waist level. The connection requires perfect timing; after contact, let the racket follow through to the left of your body.

6.   The follow-through phase should be smooth, unforced, with a slightly lifting motion. Put your weight into the follow-through. In the end you should be facing the net.

7.   Get once more into the "ready" position, so that you're prepared for the next return. Be light on your feet.

The above instructions are reversed for left-handers, of course. And keep in mind that in the heat of a tennis battle, some of the motions will have to be abbreviated.

The forehand is simpler than any description. One Florida pro just asks his students to whisper to themselves, "Back, pause, stroke!" Some of the Floridian's colleagues boil the stroke down to four words: "back, bounce, step, hit."

Tennis schools have worked out an excellent method for teaching the forehand stroke in a few lessons. Some teachers may suggest that you first go through the motions without a racket. Other schools let you use the racket but no balls for the first forehand swings.

Are the correct movements really so important? One proof comes from observing the international stars; many of them actually complete "shadow forehands" before a match and during pauses. On the courts of various resort hotels, in clubs and clinics, instructors patiently toss balls toward the beginner's racket face. A hand-thrown ball is naturally more gentle, and allows better control by a novice. This practice is later followed by racket-propelled forehand. Some instructors teach footwork separately.

At various tennis clinics for recreational players, the experts use imagery to impart correct stroking. Don Kerbis, well known for his imaginative Midwestern tennis clinics, compares the forehand drive to a "swinging garden gate." (Your shoulder is the hinge while the arm is the gate.) Instructors employ the term "a penny on edge." (Your racket stays perpendicular on the forehand stroke so that if you were to place a penny on the edge of the frame it would stay on the edge.) One West Coast teacher explains the forehand swing as "sweeping the crumbs off the table." A bad follow-through is seen as "swatting flies," and getting ready to hit the next forehand requires a "batter's stance." (The position of the feet and body alignment in hitting a forehand resembles that of a baseball batter waiting for a pitch.) At the Vic Braden "Tennis Colleges," the staff follows a comprehensive lesson program. Some valuable excerpts follow:

*Your left and right shoulders turn toward the back fence automatically as you begin your backswing pivot. This places your left side toward the net.

*Your backswing is begun the instant you have detected the direction of your opponent's shot. The initial eye level backswing is made at full speed. If you're early at this point, you may wait until it's time to begin the dropping motion.

*The racket goes back at eye level and away from your body, drops to a position approximately twelve inches below the level of the intended point of impact with the ball, and makes a low to high forward motion while striking the ball.

*Contact with the ball is made even with the left side of the body and the elbow is approximately six–ten inches away in a slightly bent position.

*The swing should be continuous until completed. This continuous motion takes advantage of the extra power gained through additional stroking lengths and the "dead weight" fall of the racket.

*Your follow-through ends by pointing toward the target and skyward at about a 20- to 30-degree angle.

These instructions cannot possibly succeed at once. Initially, tennis players make the same traditional mistakes in their forehand drives. Here are the major ones:

1.   The player fails to strike from a sideways position. Instead, the swing is made from a front (or ready) stance. Result: the ball goes out.

2.   Although in proper sideways position, the player hits at the wrong moment. The flaw may stem from bad timing or from not concentrating on the ball. Results: (a) no ball-racket connection at all (ball very far in front); (b) ball goes astray to extreme left (hit too soon); (c) ball veers out to the right (hit too late).

3. The player doesn't bring the racket back sufficiently. Too short a backswing means too-little drive. Result: the ball goes into the net.

4. The player is too close to the ball. Instead of stepping forward or backward or sideways, the beginner lets the ball crowd him. Result: not enough room to swing and a stunted "go-anywhere" flight.

5. The player makes ball contact with a loose wrist. Result: the ball flies erratically.

6. The player attempts a forehand stroke with the racket tilted too much downward or opened too much toward the sky. Result: the ball goes into the net or takes a high trajectory, which may even go over the back fence.

Your form still leaves something to be desired if your forehand strokes are awkward and cramped, if you push your racket in front of your body instead of making a long free swing at your side, if you put the *wrong* foot forward so that you are off balance when you hit the ball.

At some summer camps, the staff carefully observes these mistakes, which are noted on a special sheet for study purposes. A few tennis camps send the information to a youngster's parents.

# THE BACKHAND

Beginners often complain about the difficulty of learning the backhand, which means hitting on the left side of your body. Some people actually try to avoid this important stroke altogether and attempt to cover a court exclusively with forehands. This is difficult. A similar situation exists in Ping Pong. A player will never gain complete control of the table until he masters both backhand and forehand.

The backhand takes longer to acquire, but after enough practice, it usually becomes a tennis player's stronger stroke. Some world-class competitors deliver a greater punch with their backhands, which are more feared than their forehands. For the recreational player, the backhand is essential; without it, he remains a perennial novice.

(Forehand)

Photos 1–5. Left shoulder and hitting arm turn back simultaneously
Photo 6. Arrow shows maximum backswing for slow ball—shorter backswing a must
for fast balls

Copyright © 1972 Phil Bath—Vic Braden

Photos 8–10. Vertical racket face reaches position lower than point of impact—
produces topspin
Photos 9–13. Synchronized knee and body lift raises ball over net with topspin

(Backhand)

Photos 1–5. Right shoulder and racket arm turn back simultaneously
Photos 8–10. Circular backswing reaches position lower than intended point of impact

Copyright © 1972 Phil Bath—Vic Braden

Photos 10–12. Synchronized knee and body lift raises ball over net with topspin
Photos 11–13. Racket face is vertical and follows ball to target
Photos 14–16. Follow-through remains on line to target—body fully extended upward and outward

Instructors may suggest the following sequence for your backhand:

1.   Change from the "Eastern" forehand grip to the backhand grip by shifting your hand one-quarter turn to the left. This brings the hand on top of the narrow side of the handle, with your thumb wrapped around the grip.

2.   Turn your right shoulder toward the opponent. Your body now faces the left fence. The right toe should point diagonally toward the sideline at about twelve inches in front of your left foot. Bend the knees a bit and keep the heels off the ground.

3.   The instant the ball leaves the other court, your racket should be drawn back. Keep the left hand on the racket throat for stability, your weight on the left foot. Pivot waist and shoulders to the left until your back is half turned to the net. You should be watching the ball over your right shoulder, which is now a little lower than the left one.

4.   Here comes the ball! Swing forward with a straightened arm held fairly close to your trunk "as though in a sling." Simultaneously, shift your weight forward and to the right foot. The arm is still full, extended, with a slight elbow bend. You hit the ball some ten to twelve inches ahead of your right hip. Realize that high-bouncing balls make difficult backhands. So do ankle-high balls. Both require experience and skill. If possible, contact the ball at waist level.

5.   Let the racket follow through until it finishes well to your right, high above the net.

6.   End of stroke. You are facing the net. Be ready for another backhand!

You can learn these motions with greater ease by first trying them without a ball. (Irwin Hoffman, a well-known pro, persuaded his wife to practice the backhand swing in front of the mirror.)

You will become more familiar with the backhand by trying it from a stationary position. This is a nice way to start a rally from behind the base line. Take a ball into your left hand and just drop it at your left side, at about the level of your hips. As you hit the ball, you become aware that you can do so only in a sideways stance. The more you turn the right shoulder toward the alley, the greater your backhand-driving radius.

The "ball drops" may be followed by letting another player or an instructor hand-toss some balls toward your backhand side. Once you're able to return these gentle backhands, ask for some to be hit with a racket. Make a mental note of what happens. The footwork here is the exact reverse from the forehand.

A careful second-by-second analysis should enable the beginner to gain the upper hand over this important ground stroke.

Some pointers:

1.   Anticipate the route of the ball and hurry into the "platform" as fast as possible. Stay loose. Make sure that you'll have enough distance from the ball for comfortable stroking.

2.   Change the grip consciously as you swivel. After enough grip switching, the maneuver eventually becomes automatic.

3.   Keep your eyes glued to the ball while it approaches across the net.

4.   Have your racket back and ready to reach *under* the ball. Many beginners begin their "backswing" too late and thus produce a dwarfed, rushed stroke without follow-through.

5.   Standing merely sideways to the ball is not enough. Watch a good player handling a mild backhand; the turn is such that the right shoulder *blade* faces the net.

6.   Remember that a backhand requires an earlier rendezvous than the forehand. You must stroke when the ball is still ahead of your body; or at the latest, as it comes abreast with your bent knees. Novices often wait too long to connect, and therefore miss the ball altogether.

7.   Hit with a slight upward continuous motion. (Some instructors say "Sweep the ball over the net" or "Pretend that you're throwing your arms across the net.") During the stroke, the body weight must be transferred from the left to the right foot and *into* the ball. A faulty weight shift (backward instead of forward) or wrong footwork produce inaccurate, inadequate backhands.

Attention also must be paid to your wrist, arm, and shoulder. Have a playing partner *watch* as you make a "shadow" swing. Are you in a sideways stance? Are you using the shoulder and arm? Or are you just letting the elbow do all the work? If so, you may risk an inflammation. Is the arm solid? Is your wrist rigid, as it should be for the stroke?

Wrist flexibility is essential for the serve, but you drive a backhand with a locked wrist. This is especially important for beginners. The evidence comes to us from films that show how much force a ball exerts against the racket. Unless the wrist is set to withstand this force, the racket will "give," and a split-second's yielding diminishes your drive power, changes the angle of your racket strings, and catapults the ball into the wrong direction. Young women and children are frequent victims of this weakness because they lack the wrist strength to control their tennis rackets. One way to achieve more rigidity: squeeze the racket handle at the moment of ball impact. This momentarily reinforces the wrist, resisting the force of the ball and adding control.

Top players have such excellent timing that a slight flick accomplishes

The instructor shows a pupil the correct elbow position for the backhand. The elbow need not be locked. *Photo courtesy Don Kerbis Tennis Schools.*

surprise hits, and last-instant direction changes. Tennis stars must conceal the flight of a backhand drive until the last moment, and they do so with a wristy motion. But not every player is quick enough or talented enough to break the rigid-wrist-stroking rule.

The problem even has plagued some otherwise capable tournament players. Despite superb strokes and strategy, one young competitor had an especially bad time with his wrist. He had a manufacturer invent a special metal bracelet, which would let him serve, yet assure firmness for his backhands and forehands. The band was delivered, and the man trained with it for several months.

One day he was finally ready for a major match.

The umpire cited the rules. The bracelet could not be worn.

The competitor had no choice but to play without it. Would he be able to deliver strokes with a firm wrist? Unfortunately, he could not. The wrist band had spoiled him. He still hadn't *consciously* acquired the rigid wrist habit. His balls went out. He lost point after point. After the first game, the man was so enraged that he smashed his new wood racket and left.

The moral is obvious. A player must learn to control every part of his body.

There is one backhand variation worth mentioning. You may have seen it used by some leading competitors, and tennis-club pros teach it regularily to small children and women. It is the "two-handed" backhand.

It means that the player holds the racket with both hands; the left hand is on the upper part of the handle, close to the throat, while the right hand is around the grip in the "Eastern" style. (The right hand does the guiding.) This "double hold" naturally adds double strength to a youngster's backhand. The wobbly wrist is eliminated and the backhand stroke is easier to learn. Some of the drawbacks sometimes show up when a person reaches the advanced tennis ranks. At this point, a two-fisted backhand can lessen arm mobility, and cause slight stroking limitations. World-class competitors are such good athletes, however, that they know how to eliminate or compensate for some of the disadvantages. Many recreational players eventually change to the regular backhand.

The forehand and backhand series of photographs are designed to demonstrate the use of the fence as a teaching technique. Starting from the "ready position" next to the fence, Irwin Hoffman shows the correct backswing and follow-through positions for both the ground strokes. In both the forehand and backhand the stroking motion covers one hemisphere or half circle. Both strokes begin below the ball and finish above it. By positioning himself next to the fence, Irwin restricts the tendency to exaggerate the backswing and follow-through. *Photos by Ed Reed, Heather Ridge Racket Club, Denver, Colorado.*

CHAPTER 5

Ken Rosewall. *Photo by Art Seitz.*

# Serves and Returns of Serves

Forehands and backhands give you the tools for rallying. After you become more skillful with these two ground strokes, you'll keep the ball in play longer. You now want to challenge someone and keep score.

At this juncture, the ability to *serve* becomes vital.

Some basic service proficiency is expected among weekend players on public courts, in tennis clubs, or when you face a fellow resort guest across the net. Most tennis people demand adequate (though not necessarily perfect) serving. More experienced players, while courteous enough not to refuse a set, tactfully shun those who cannot get the ball into a service court most of the time. Many instructors and competitors consider the serve the most important shot in tennis.

In a game, you get two chances before losing a point. The second failure to deliver the ball into the forecourt is called a "double fault." Too many double faults make you lose, of course. In fact, if two persons possess equally strong ground strokes, and are both fit and intelligent, the *service* will tip the scales. The better server probably wins the match. Learning to serve *well*, therefore, deserves a time investment.

Most instructors recommend that novices start off with the "Eastern" forehand grip for the service; later on, the student graduates to a handle position between forehand and backhand. Some players, including most top players, choose to serve with a backhand grip. (See previous chapter for details.)

The stance for the service is standard.

Stand a few inches behind the base line. When serving in a singles game to the left court, stand about a foot to the right of the center. A service to the left court requires a position one or more feet to the right of the base line's center. (You always serve cross court.)

Remember to keep both feet behind the line. You cannot step over the base line and into your court before hitting the ball.

If you step on or over the baseline and touch the ground before your racket meets the ball, you commit a foot fault, which is illegal. You then lose the point.

Remember that during the serve, your left foot (which is in front) remains stationary. Use the position you adopted for the forehand: you're sideways to the net with shoulders lined up in the direction the ball will travel. The feet are spread from twelve to twenty inches (about shoulder width) depending on the player's height. Before you attempt to toss and then hit the ball into your opponent's forecourt, some other details must be observed. Vic Braden, inventor of the "tennis colleges" sums up each item:

> (a) Your racket is pointing toward the service court, (b) your left hand is holding a tennis ball while lightly cradling the racket at the throat, (c) your left shoulder points toward the left net post, (d) your left foot points toward the right net post and is approximately one inch behind the baseline, (e) your right foot is comfortably spread behind the left foot parallel to the baseline, (f) your shoulders, arms, and body are relaxed, and (g) your body rests over both feet.

You're now ready for an important part of the service.

The toss. A great deal depends on it. Lay the racket aside for the initiation. Begin with one ball cupped in the fingertips of your outstretched left hand. (Keep your elbow firm.) Lift your hand from waist level to about the height of the shoulders and let your fingers release the ball. Some instructors emphasize that you should not pitch it, but merely *lift* it, so that it "floats" upward.

The description fits. Only a slight toss will make the ball descend gently and slowly; this gives you an extra instant for the serve. It is also important that the ball should not be sent up too high, or gravity will bring it down with too much force. Besides, a moving object is harder to hit, and you do try to hit the ball before it falls. On the other extreme, you cannot toss too low if you want to achieve the correct slant. How high should the toss go? Most teachers suggest that the service-contact point should be no higher than twenty-five to twenty-seven inches above your uplifted wrist. You should toss to the highest point within reach of your racket. Eventually, you'll exceed this altitude by stretching still further or, as competitors do, by leaping. But even for advanced players, the toss should go *straight* up, and not at an angle.

Your eyes must follow the round object after it leaves your palm and "balloons" upward. The throw is best directed slightly to the right, and at an arm's length in front of you. Try it first minus your racket: the ball should bounce next to the right foot. This may be more difficult than a beginner expects. Irwin Hoffman, who directed tennis schools for two decades in the West, worked out an interesting practice gimmick for his service apprentices. He made them heave the ball so that it would come down into a laundry basket. As Hoffman's pupils progressed, they'd "graduate" to a pail. The veteran instructor considered these preparations important enough to suggest five hundred to one thousand practice tosses a week. Other teachers will let you catch the trial balls in your open hand.

It is worth knowing that, during a match, you need only serve if the toss is satisfactory. You can therefore repeat the throwing process without penalty. (On the other hand, you lose a point if you try to hammer the ball down but make no connection.)

All this effort makes sense, because you need a perfect toss to bring about a perfect service swing. You practice the latter with your racket in the right hand and two balls in the left one (if you're right-handed). Your racket arm now sweeps back and up, bends for a moment at the elbow; the racket almost touching your back, then smoothly making its second ascent to contact the ball. The upward and forward striking motion is made with a flexible, "snapping" wrist and a straightened arm. (It is impossible to serve with a stiff wrist.) During this final phase, the chin remains up and the eyes still focus on the ball. At the point of impact, the racket is extended to the apex of one's reach. A split-second after ball contact, the right foot must step forward. (This brings your body weight forward, too.) The server's racket is aimed in the direction of the other court.

Most people precede the whole business by bouncing the ball a few times against their (horizontal) strings. This bouncing reminds one of a basketball player getting the feel for his ball and starting a rhythm.

Some tennis players develop a fairly adequate serve without the initial first swing; they start with the bent elbow and the racket-gripping knuckles close to the back of the neck. This is called a "hammer and nail" serve, and many schools start out beginners with it. One Australian woman competitor seems to get along with this "back-scratching" half of a serve. But the introductory motion adds power, and almost all competitors and advanced players depend on the complete swing. In any case, the ball should not be "pushed" patty-cake fashion across the net but pulled down over the net from the highest reachable point above one's head. The correct wrist motion resembles that of a throwing baseball pitcher. Male servers often make the error of putting out too much force. They "lay in the big bomb" and try to deliver cannonballs, Arthur Ashe style. This is a mistake, of course. The first serves should strive only for accuracy, and not power. Control is more important than speed, and the hard-hit balls may go out. Instructors say that you should be able to get seven of ten services into the proper court.

It actually takes thousands of serves to achieve consistent control. It also takes a fierce concentration and a fine coordination to serve well. Watch a pro like Rosie Casals (who first studied ballet) or Roscoe Tanner, one of the male

Copyright © 1972 Phil Bath—Vic Braden

(Serve front view)

Photo 1. Swing begins near waist level —body relaxed

Photos 1–6. Both arms are dropped simultaneously

Photos 6–9. Shown is advanced service toss with ball throwing arm parallel to base line to facilitate greater shoulder turn—beginners toss from front side

Photos 9–10. Fingers open for ball toss when arm parallel to ground

Photos 11–20. Loopswing behind back is formed by relaxed elbow—shoulders roll forward ahead of arm swing

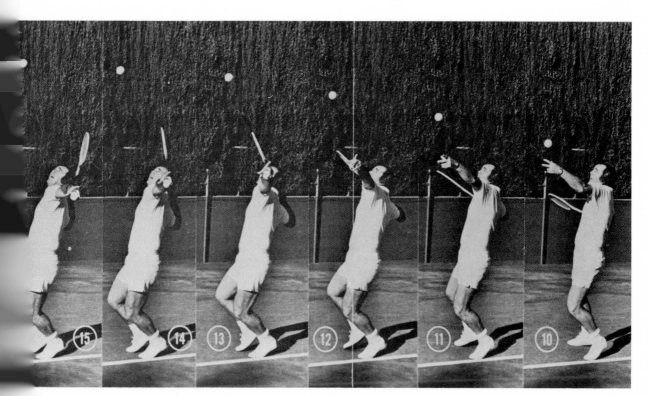

Photos 21–24. Hitting motion is upward and forward—eyes focus on the ball—chin
up

Copyright © 1972 Phil Bath—Vic Braden

Photos 23–27. Wrist is loose while snapping
Photos 28–35. Follow-through is to left of body facilitating easy shoulder roll

On the serve, hit the ball as high as you can hold your racket. Using serving device. *Photo by Hagood.*

specialists. Their services are fluid, continuous, rhythmic, effortless, and beautiful to look at. Top-class players develop such a well-oiled service that they generate ball speeds of 100 to 125 miles per hour. (The world record hovers near 150 mph.) Despite the quick uncoiling and a split-second contact, double faults are kept to a minimum. The ball generally lands on target. The champion can "ace" an opponent who will be able to return the ball.

By contrast, the Sunday player often overshoots the service line or discovers that the net is much too high. His shots come in "wide" and land in the doubles alleys.

At least three major service problems can be corrected with some adjustments:

| PROBLEM | REASON | REMEDY |
|---|---|---|
| You're overserving (ball goes too far). | Toss may be too high or wrist not flexible enough. | Toss farther toward net or lower toss. |
| Ball is falling too short (into net). | Toss is too low, ball too far in front, or you're hitting down on ball. | Toss higher, swing upward and forward. |
| Ball is sometimes too short, sometimes too long. | Erratic toss. | Watch your toss pattern and change accordingly. |

Some beginners serve too softly; they deliver "fuzz sandwiches," "love pats," or "helium balls," as instructors jokingly say. Gentle services put beginners at a better opponent's mercy; the return then becomes so much easier.

The flaw can be corrected by putting your weight into the serve to increase speed. Hit above your head from right to left in a downward hammer motion. Many persons eventually manage to toss correctly, then to bring the body weight into the serve and deliver the ball in the service area. An advanced player usually aims for the other person's backhand, especially on second serve (unless the adversary has a weak forehand!). Corners make good targets, "pulling" the receiver toward one side, making him vulnerable to the ball aimed into the other part of his court. Pros serve so precisely that they hit a wood block or a handkerchief at will. Their service stroke is so nearly perfect that they can direct the ball to any point on the forecourt, including the gap between the other person's feet.

Moreover, experienced players learn how to vary their service by varying the toss. In this manner, they can surprise and outwit an opponent, who

On the serve, showing use of the restrictive platform, an innovation of Mrs. Grafton. This platform holds the back foot down, giving the student the feel of using the hand and wrist in the upward and downward motion for control and speed. Too many pupils throw the right hip forward before hitting the ball. *Photo by Hagood.*

The student should hold onto the ball as long as possible for control. Look up the left arm for the height of the throw. Too low or too high a toss can both result in inaccurate serves. *Photo by Hagood.*

never knows what to expect. (Another school of thought that applies to advanced players: you keep an identical toss but vary the racket position on contact. This last-second adjustment won't give the receiver enough time to guess the intent of your service.)

A beginner has no need to disguise serves or to serve in a manner that may damage his shoulder. He gets along well with a "flat" service. It begins with a toss slightly to the right and in front. Todd Harris, a Florida resident pro, explains the tosses and various serves to his more advanced students by means of a big clock. "I ask them to stand almost sideways to the net," Harris says. "I suggest that they imagine a big clock facing them over their left shoulder. If they toss the ball somewhere between twelve and one on the face of the clock, they create a 'flat' serve. Toss to the eight or nine is for a *twist* serve. Toss to the three for a 'slice.'

First-class competitors also change the speed, pace, and direction of a serve, with each serve planned carefully in advance. A powerful service that wins a point (an "ace") often "psyches" the other player.

Good servers can cope with special problems. The most common ones can be handled as follows:

1. *The sun*  A bright sun need not faze you while serving. Try to look elsewhere. Position your head in such a manner that the sun is not in your eyes. (Your body slant does not change; you just use peripheral vision.)

2. *Wind*  Extra power is needed if the wind blows against you, and you must hit into it. As you serve, your toss should be farther in front than normally. If the wind comes from behind, it will carry the ball into the other court. Beware of throwing too far in front then; serve more lightly and take a shorter aim.

## RETURN OF SERVES

There are individuals with a knack for serving, while others are quick and steady with their return of serves. The serious tennis player tries to develop excellence in both.

The return of a serve begins with the "ready" position. Your knees are bent and apart. The racket is held like a gun toward your opponent diagonally across from you. The "ready" stance allows skipping sideways and running forward; the racket can be swung left for a backhand or to the right for a forehand.

Where should the receiver stand in a singles game? It depends on the server's ability. If you face another novice, his serve probably will land gently, if at all. You can therefore post yourself behind the base line, to the left of the singles boundary line. This location permits you to cover the whole right service court.

As the game begins, and the other person serves a number of times, the receiver can choose a spot further back. Competitors usually wait for the unleashed cannonballs far behind the base line.

Keep in mind that most players' first serves are more powerful than the second ones. If the ball goes out, the experienced server will be more cautious with the second service. He must avoid a double fault, which would be a free point for you. The second serve therefore may be shorter, which means that you, too, should be closer to the net.

Perfect return of service requires perfect concentration. Keep your eyes glued to the server's ball. Watch it being heaved and struck. This is so crucial that some tennis stars admit that, as they wait for service, they sometimes talk to themselves. "Watch the ball! Watch the ball!"

The alertness pays off; some servers are telegraphing the path and landing point of their balls. This knowledge enables you to return it.

A player who anticipates the flight of a ball usually also can skip, hop, or run toward it, get into position, and bring back his arm for the return. The expert's racket is in position before the approaching ball clears the net. If he doesn't have time to turn sideways, he will at least swivel his shoulders. Very hard and swift serves require more anticipation.

Clark Graebner.
*Photo by Art Seitz.*

How do you predetermine the path of a ball? It depends on how you hold your racket during the return of serve. A slight slant toward the sun, like the windshield of a car, causes your ball return to fly high. (The more horizontal your racket face, the higher it sails.) The opposite happens if you hold the racket downward; the more you do so, the lower the ball will go.

Slow services are the most pleasant ones. The receiver can employ a regular, carefully grooved forehand or backhand. A power serve leaves too little time for such niceties; your backswing has to be shortened. Some gifted beginners accidentally discover the abbreviated return. They chop, chip, and cut the ball, which possesses enough impetus to clear the net and land in the court of their dynamic opponent. Sometimes a short backswing may be coupled with a long follow-through. Service returns should be made a little farther in front of the body than regular returns.

Experienced receivers hop from their ready position into a bouncy light-footedness, but they stop long enough for a "platform." They drive a ball on the run only in emergencies.

Even after playing for several decades, some people know their own limitations, and they won't attempt impossible shots or shots beyond their capacity, but simply strive for control. Competitors avoid giving away points with careless service returns; at the same time, they try to make placements calculated to win a game. The following are their most effective returns of service:

1.  Down the line (deep)
2.  Cross court (away from the server; or short)
3.  At the server's feet, if he rushes the net
4.  Over the head of a server who rushes the net
5.  To the opponent's special weakness

Chapter 7 will treat these competitive refinements in greater detail.

# PART THREE
## Tennis Techniques
## for Better Players

# CHAPTER 6

# Refinements: Volleys, Lobs, and Smashes

A tennis player soon realizes that the two basic ground strokes must be complemented by other shots. There is the "volley," which means hitting a ball *before* it bounces. There are the "lobs" that propel a ball in an arc over an opponent's head. The beginner stage ends by learning the "smash," where the ball is reached above the head and rammed into the other court (hence the name "overhead"). An experienced tennis player's arsenal includes the "drop shot"; it refers to a ball dropped lightly across the net. "Half volleys" are balls bouncing low, which you hit immediately. To handle them requires a deep knee bend and utmost concentration. Experience will also teach that balls can be made to spin through the air in various ways and directions.

Whatever shot he grapples with, a pro looks smooth. Economy of movement is one reason. Even an average person should therefore think in terms of simplifying motions. Small skipping steps are best, and it is advisable to avoid hectic running and jumping. A teacher can judge someone's tennis level by how good he or she looks. How does the player step toward the ball? How calm is the person while stroking? Are the motions consistently deliberate and sure, or is the player almost always off balance and leaping too much?

Erratic playing fatigues faster, and the lack of balance creates a lack of control.

Before "graduating" to the more advanced tennis shots, a player should also become aware of the various spins and their applications. While the "spin" seems at first accidental, it becomes important in match play. A weekend competitor can gain points by adding one of several rotations to a ball, which changes its pace and direction.

In Vic Braden's "Tennis Colleges," the spins are categorized and characterized as follows:

1.  *Topspin* refers to a ball that is spinning forward from a side view, at a 90-degree vertical angle. Topspin generates a downward force. A ball hit with topspin will generally resemble the arc of the rainbow, while staying within a directional track. Some topspin uses:

* Safe shots from base line
* As offensive lobs
* For safe serves
* For some overhead shots
* To make a ball drop at netman's feet

2.  *Sidespin* refers to a ball rotating *(counterclockwise),* from a side view, on a 180-degree horizontal plane. Sidespin generates a curve ball, which carries shorter distances and moves quickly out of a directional track. Some sidespin uses:

* For serves that pull opponents "out of court" or for outright "aces"
* Occasionally a player uses a slight sidespin shot made on the run toward the net.
* For volleys

3. *Underspin or backspin* refers to a ball turning counterclockwise, from a side view, at a 90-degree vertical angle. Until gravity controls the ball, underspin generates an upward force, and an inverted rainbow arc. Some underspin uses:

* To keep your shots skidding. This forces your opponent to hit from a low position.
* For change of pace
* For drop shots
* For safe, deep, floating defensive backhands from base line

# THE VOLLEY

"Volleying" means returning a ball before it has bounced; a player volleys behind the net or while en route to the net. The mastery of this shot

Charlene Grafton and Wes Overton show how they hit through the oval to improve precision volleying. *Photo by Hagood.*

(Volley forehand)

Photos 1–4. Left shoulder turns body for short backswing
Photos 5–9. Body moves forward to meet ball—eyes focused on ball—eyes at impact
level

Copyright © 1972 Phil Bath—Vic Braden

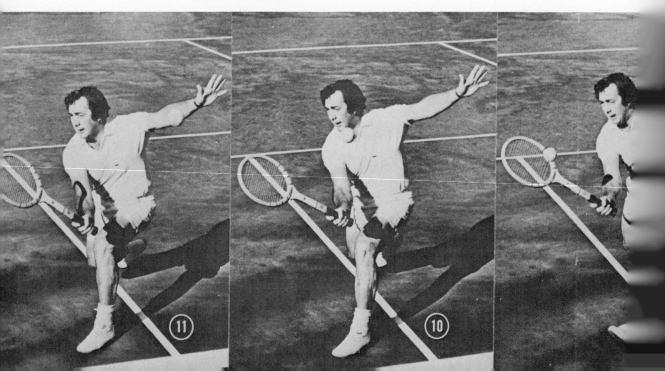

Photos 1–11. Racket head remains higher than wrist level
Photo 8. Tighten fingers before ball contacts racket
Photos 8–11. Palm of hitting hand faces target throughout stroke
Photo 11. Follow-through short for beginners

(Volley backhand)

Photos 1–5. Switch to backhand grip as right shoulder turns racket arm for backswing
Photos 1–14. Racket head remains above wrist level—knees lower body—eyes at impact level

Copyright © 1972 Phil Bath—Vic Braden

Photo 11. Hitting arm is fully extended at impact
Photos 10–14. Knuckles of hitting hand point to target—short follow-through for
        beginners

has several advantages, most of which are of a strategic nature. For one thing, the person close to the net can control a wide area and make placements at will. A volley provides command over the court; one can strike swiftly and at all angles. Volleying skills prove important for the doubles game, where much of the action takes place in the forecourts. In both doubles and singles, the volley is a good weapon against those who hug the base line. The net offers a psychological advantage: you can intimidate an opponent there. Whether delivered as backhands or forehands, volleys can be effective only if you're aggressive. The motion itself has been frequently compared with that of a fencer or boxer. The tennis player steps forward quickly, with the wrist as firm as possible.

A beginner has to summon courage to play close to the net. Some people fear that they will get hurt by a ball. This happens all too seldom. A volleyer almost instinctively uses his racket as a shield. It is true that you need experience at the net; the balls fly faster there than at the base line, by which time they can decelerate. Everything happens quickly up front, and if you don't watch out, the other person can shoot past you. Good vision and reflexes, therefore, are needed. Seniors often prefer to operate from the back courts instead.

In the hands of an expert, the volley becomes a sharp tool for earning points.

Most recreational players require much practice. They can get it by first asking their partners to throw and then hit easy balls into the air. The volleyer gets into position behind the net while the other person stands in the service court, feeding him balls. At some tennis clinics, several students return the ball to an instructor, who keeps it in play by means of volleys.

Some people continue to use the Eastern forehand grip for all volleying, whether it is done in front, to the left, or to the right. Instructors may suggest a grip somewhat between the finger and palm positions of the forehand and backhand. The majority of competitiors utilize one grip for both forehand and backhand volleys. They place the palm halfway between an Eastern forehand and an Eastern backhand grip. The major argument is that the net doesn't give much time to change your hand's position on the racket handle. One hold can therefore be best, especially for beginners who don't want to think of too many things—grip, hands, and feet—at the same time.

Net play requires only slight force; a punch usually suffices.

The basis for the volley is your "ready position." As always, your feet are apart, knees flexed, racket steadied with the free hand. Although you face the net, your left shoulder should be slightly ahead for the forehand volley (right shoulder for the backhand). Think of both as abbreviated ground strokes that demand almost no backswing and very little follow-through. (Most players swing too hard.) Ideally, the weight is always on the forward foot, your left eye for the forehand volley, the right one for the backhand. Keep the racket above the net.

Volleying takes no strength. The player profits from the momentum and drive of the approaching ball. If it comes with great force, he need merely be there and block it. A slower ball can be "punched." The hitter always leans slightly forward. It is sensible to strike at an *undefended* part of the opposite court.

Volleys are normally hit in front of the body, with the racket raised somewhat higher than for the ground stroke. If a ball comes straight at you across the net, take it with a backhand volley.

A "half volley" is the term for a low, defensive volley, usually made from behind the net. Despite its name, a half volley bounces first. You bend the knees to make such a shot. Contortions from the waist don't work. Because

A two-handed backhand volley is executed to perfection by Chris Evert.

the ball may have to be scooped up inches from the ground, you have less time to execute a half volley than an average ground stroke. Good balance and concentration are vital for this tricky maneuver.

# LOBS, SMASHES, AND OTHER SHOTS

The "lob" is a ball that rises steeply, sails over your rival's head, and then plummets behind him. The best lobs land "deep" in the other's territory, close to the base line. Such shots can get your opponent *into* trouble—he may have to run far for the ball—and at the same time get you *out* of trouble. You dispatch lobs to ward off too much net rushing, for instance. Your tactic forces the adversary backward and, at least for the moment, removes the threat at the net.

Lobs can be beneficial when you're out of position or find yourself in a corner with too large an area to defend. In these instances, a sky-high lob will keep the other party busy and give you a few extra seconds to achieve a better stance or hurry to a better location.

Tennis pros historically distinguish between offensive and defensive lobs. Here are the classic definitions:

*Defensive lobs are hit as high as twenty-five feet over the net with the primary purpose of buying more time to regain a lost position, to hit over the head of an opposing volleyer, and to sometimes simply change the pace.

*Offensive lobs are balls hit just high enough to be out of the reach of the other net player. Such lobs clear the net by about fifteen feet. The objective is to win points outright. The offensive lob also allows you to take the net position yourself while the rival chases the ball to the base line.

Beginners will find it almost natural to lob well, especially with their stronger ground stroke (usually the forehand). The racket should be open, with a 45 percent slant on ball contact. The customary hard drive becomes unnecessary; you lob with a looping, spooning, slightly lifting motion and a long follow-through. Too much power will make the lob wind up beyond the base line. Teachers say that one should aim high at first, forcing the ball to climb at a 70-degree angle.

Lobbing is not considered heroic; a male may not cut a dashing figure when he sends up too many of these flares. Nevertheless, even tennis stars get out of jams that way, and new netters would be wise to acquire the skill. One tennis technician sums it up intelligently and amusingly for us: "The lob is like religion. It has few vocal supporters, but few care to attack it in print; it is practiced comparatively little, yet people turn to it in moments of need."

Some lobbing pointers:

*Practice at first with a partner.

*It's better to lob too high and too long instead of too low and too short.

*Put topspin on the ball to control distance.

*Propel a high lob with underspin so that you have time to get back into court.

*Keep your knees bent. Your eyes should be riveted to the ball.

*Hit all lobs from below the waist level. Get under the ball and keep it on your strings as long as possible.

While you learn to lob, your fellow player can practice smashing the ball and learn "overheads." This advanced stroke becomes essential for competitors.

An "overhead" or "smash" may be one of tennis' most difficult shots.

To strike a high, descending ball takes split-second timing, coordination, touch, and supreme confidence. Yet it is desirable to work at this shot until it becomes part of your repertoire. Even then, you may not succeed in making contact each time. When you do, you'll feel a great sense of achievement. The smash is dramatic to watch, and a deadly put-away shot in a tournament. Instructors teach it because you need overheads to play in singles matches and in doubles games. The smash is the only logical reply to a lob or to other easy, high balls.

Students often wonder if they should let the ball bounce and *then* hit it. The answer: smash most balls before they have a chance to come down. Once you can smash well, you'll give the other player less time for return. Allow only the highest or deepest lobs to bounce first.

Technically, the overhead is often compared to the serve. You use the same grip; you hit the ball at the same height as you do in a service. The overhead swing resembles that of the service, too, except that the motions must be shortened for lack of time. Some players use abbreviated backswings or bring the racket back between their shoulder blades and then strike.

Here's the exact sequence for an efficient smash:

1.   Take long steps to get to the striking area, and short, quick steps to position yourself perfectly.

2.   Turn sideways, left shoulder forward, right elbow bent, racket head high against your spine.

3.   Your left arm points at the ball, hand and fingers extended. This lowers your right shoulder.

4.   Now swing upward and forward and hit the ball above your head with a flexible wrist and a straight arm. Swing *through* the ball.

5.   Keep your chin up during the entire process, including the servicelike windup. Look up; if you look down, your stroke may be faulty, with an incomplete follow-through. The motion is continuous from beginning to end, like a serve.

Beginners sometimes try for a smash when they should not do so; a forehand stroke would probably be safer. It is no good to attempt slamming neck-high balls; such smashes will not go over unless you're near the net.

Overhead training should begin only after you can serve well. Begin with easy smashes; the ball should be up and well in front of you. Don't hit too softly; many eager beavers thrash the racket down too *hard,* so that the shot ends up in their own courts. Avoid the spectacular Rod Laver jumps; leaping will just draw you out of balance. The beginner is better off to let some of the balls bounce before hitting. No need to copy world-class competitors who will take nine out of ten smashes right out of the sky.

(Overhead smash)

Photo 1. Reach quickly—begin backswing immediately
Photos 1–8. A time-saver—racket head on backswing is chest level
Photos 9–13. Loop behind back is same as service motion

Copyright © 1972 Phil Bath—Vic Braden

Photos 14–17. Swing upward and forward to meet ball
Photos 17–19. Overhead hits from deep court position require topspin for control
Photos 18–25. Weight is transferred forward during hitting motion

Apart from overheads, an expert's arsenal contains a deceptively gentle maneuver that is called "drop shot."

"Drop shots" are delicate ground strokes made from the forecourt. The ball will parachute almost directly behind the net, making the other player rush and strain to reach it.

Here are the mechanics:

1.   Watch the ball. Get your racket under it and stroke lightly. Most beginners use too much force.

2.   Hold the handle lightly; tightening does not produce an appropriate shot.

John Newcombe. *Photo by Art Seitz.*

3.   Limit your backswing and use almost no follow-through. This is the only way to get a low bounce behind the net.

The drop-shot strategy should be used mostly for surprise and as a change of pace. You can use this shot only if the opponent is far away from the net, and if he happens to be a slow runner.

A ball first must bounce before you can make a drop shot. In addition, you can take the ball directly out of the air. A slight upward blocking movement with a firm wrist will produce the so-called "drop volley." Professionals are able to estimate the power of any ball, and can therefore make drop volleys from back courts. The most effective shots travel toward an opponent's weaker side. This is usually his backhand. You also drop-volley to an area that forces him to run far and exhaust himself.

If these specialty shots miss their target and go into a back court instead, chances are that the ball will be fired back as a winner.

# CHAPTER 7

Arthur Ashe. *Photo courtesy Las Vegas News Bureau.*

# Becoming an Effective Singles Player

A prominent Florida tennis instructor used to say that every player thinks "that he is better than he really is." A beginner would be unrealistic to assume that he has acquired enough competence to play an outstanding singles match. He first requires adequate stroke production and enough "ball control" to place a ball reliably anywhere on the other court. This skill comes after numerous lessons and practice sessions over a period of months.

Instructors also point to certain drills, some of which can be done alone:

*Bounce the ball fifty to seventy times from waist level to the ground.
*Work on movement fundamentals with the racket:
a.—Pivot—step—swing.
b.—Pivot right—slide—step forward—swing.

    c.—Pivot left—slide—step forward—swing.

    d.—Step directly forward—pivot left—step diagonally back—right step forward—left swing.

    *Practice overhead throwing motion without ball. Stand seven to ten feet away from the wall with 36-inch-high line marked on it representing a net.

    *Practice a complete service motion with your racket only.

    *Serve a bushel of old tennis balls into the proper court. Pick up the balls and repeat diagonally until you've hit two hundred services. (Concentrate each time before serving.)

You should also practice with a partner. Try the following well-known drills:

    *Hit twenty-five consecutive balls over net from the base line, twenty-five off forehand, and twenty-five off backhand.

    *Hit twenty-five consecutive balls forehand cross court (from one corner to opposite corner).

    *Bounce and hit fifteen consecutive lobs.

    *Hit twenty out of twenty-five balls into right service court, then into the left.

    *Volley twenty-five balls fed to you at the net by a partner.

    *Hit ten times accurately in a straight line (known as "down the line").

    *Serve accurately five or more times. Keep serving until you achieve the desired number. (The partner can return ball.)

    *Return partner's serves with an emphasis of clearing the net by four to ten feet. "Net skimming" is a dangerous practice for intermediates.

You may want to take a cue from tennis schools, and make a written record that will reveal and underline your weaknesses. One of the most intriguing "tennis error" charts is used by the Kerbis Indoor Tennis Club in Illinois. Every mistake is carefully recorded by the instructor, who thereby speeds up a player's progress. The chart looks like this:

| TYPE OF ERROR | FOREHAND | BACKHAND | FOREHAND VOLLEY | BACKHAND VOLLEY | OVERHEAD |
|---|---|---|---|---|---|
| Hit over baseline | | | | | |
| Hit into net | | | | | |
| Missed cross court | | | | | |
| Missed down line | | | | | |
| Court position | | | | | |
| | NETTED | NETTED | SHALLOW | HIGH | ACED |
| Return of service | | | | | |

| THE SERVE | RIGHT COURT | LEFT COURT | TOTAL | PERCENTAGE |
|---|---|---|---|---|
| Total number serves | | | | |
| Good first serves | | | | |
| Good second serves | | | | |
| Double faults | | | | |
| Comments: | | | | |

At the Cliff Buchholz Tennis School, in Colorado, the student analysis sheets give an excellent clue to your progress. Here is what the instructors look for:

| FUNDAMENTAL | FOREHAND | | | BACKHAND | | | F. H. VOLLEY | | | B. H. VOLLEY | | |
|---|---|---|---|---|---|---|---|---|---|---|---|---|
| | POOR | FAIR | GOOD | POOR | FAIR | GOOD | POOR | FAIR | GOOD | POOR | FAIR | GOOD |
| Watch the ball | | | | | | | | | | | | |
| Proper grips | | | | | | | | | | | | |
| Body positioning | | | | | | | | | | | | |
| Stroke preparation | | | | | | | | | | | | |
| Wrist/elbow control | | | | | | | | | | | | |
| Proper contact point | | | | | | | | | | | | |
| Body control during swing | | | | | | | | | | | | |
| Racket follow-through | | | | | | | | | | | | |
| Stroke production and form | | | | | | | | | | | | |

Accuracy
Movement and body
   coordination

How to improve weaknesses in your tennis foundation:

1.
2.
3.
4.
5.

SERVE

|  | POOR | FAIR | GOOD |
|---|---|---|---|
| Proper grips | | | |
| A proper and consistent toss | | | |
| Racket and body coordination | | | |
| Wrist and elbow snap | | | |
| Proper contact point | | | |
| Body and head control | | | |
| Accuracy | | | |
| Proper form | | | |
| Use of spins | | | |
| Second serve | | | |
| Overhead | | | |
| Lob | | | |
| Service return | | | |
| Conditioning | | | |
| Confidence | | | |
| Competition | | | |

Constant self-scrutiny should sharpen anyone's technique. Some players try hard to make changes by actually talking to themselves under their breaths. During rallys they whisper to themselves "Firm wrist!" or "Relax!" A noted woman pro worked on her singles game by focusing for five minutes on just one problem, and then on to the next. A five-minute stint could be devoted, for instance, to leaning *into* the ball while stroking. A player can focus on making proper ball contact with the racket strings, and so get fewer hits on the rim or the racket throat. The weaknesses of missing easy shots (lack of eye contact), hitting into the back fence (too much force or dropping the racket head), or shooting into the side fences (facing the net instead of being sideways to it) can all be eliminated with concentrated practice.

Ball control comes gradually. It should include the ability to serve with a minimum of double faults, the production of solid forehands, backhands and strong volleys. An adequate command of other strokes becomes the basis for worthwhile *interesting* match play.

It is good singles strategy to place a ball far away from the opponent, or to shoot at his feet. *Photo by Julie Warn.*

At this juncture, it is important to polish the arts of lobbing and hitting overheads and to learn "approach shots." Some coaches consider these essential for tournament tennis; a player must be able to hit well en route to an attack from the forecourt.

If the hitter delivers a deep and low approach shot to his opponent's backhand, he's almost certain to win the point on the next volley or overhead. If he returns a short ball with a weak approach shot, he's now at the net with very little reaction time, which places him on defense rather than offense. Approach shots require a sideways-to-the-net position, with a continuous forward lunge. Because of the short distances, almost no backswing is needed.

Some intermediates already understand the geometry of a ball's flight. They can guess the exact court spot where it should be met. Better singles players are not discouraged by difficult shots. They know that if their racket can touch a ball, they usually can return it. While they're not afraid to run, they know a knockout shot when they see one and won't exhaust themselves in its pursuit. They waste no lung power. Good players start early; their timing is excellent; and they almost always strike at the right moment. This can mean a split-second's wait before stroking. They memorize the court and can direct the ball wherever it suits them.

## FIRST MATCH PLAY

Instructors often warn that "35 percent of a tennis game will be made up of good strokes, and 65 percent of learning what to do with them."

At first, the best tactic may be to play as flawlessly as possible. Get the ball across the net with sure shots. Avoid chancey strokes. Don't try a shot you don't "own." Take no risks. Watch the ball and not the opponent. Don't try to impress the other person or blow him off the court.

Play gently at first. A Lake Tahoe, California, tennis director puts it this way: "If you can keep the ball in play four times across the net you can beat 50 percent of the people you play; if you keep it in play seven times you can beat anybody." In short, wait for the other person to make mistakes.

Eighty percent of the points are *lost* through error and not won through technical fireworks. Indeed, according to statistics, an intermediate's mistakes outnumber points won by placements twenty to one. (For the pros, the figure is ten to one.) Some examples: Don't give away any serves; your second serve *must* go in. Be defensive at first; employ your strongest strokes—the forehand, perhaps—and fight the temptation to crack spectacular (but unsuccessful) overheads. You may want to let a lob bounce for easier handling, and then bring it into your forehand or backhand radius. Don Kerbis, a noted tennis-school pioneer, always advised his students to "avoid cute shots." He admonished them to "stick to the fundamentals." It seems sensible to avoid what is known as the "killer complex." The harder one swings, the more the errors.

Many weekend players cannot turn down the opportunity to lash out at a ball, driving it wildly as they advance toward the net, where only half the force is needed. (The net puts us 50 percent closer to the other's base line!) While dashing forward, a new singles player had best *stop* before stroking or hit the ball lightly on the run. The above ideas can be summed up in three brief lines:

The more carefully you play,
The longer you will keep the ball going,
The more chances that your opponent will drop it.

Caution and steadiness should be coupled with intelligent placements. Listen to the dictates of logic, and play according to the old slogan, "Put it where the other man ain't." Look for the "sweet spot," or gap. Be alert to the other person's location; meanwhile, try to stay in the center of your own court.

Good strategy is based on sense of observation. To illustrate, let's say you notice that someone always stays back, hugging the base line. You'll probably score by sending balls into the forecourts. (For advanced "psyching," see the special chapter on competition playing.) If you detect a weak backhand, aim only into the backhand side. Serves also may be directed to the backhand and into the corners.

Keep your opponent on the move. "I wanted to make *her* run so that she didn't make *me* run," a woman champ once told the press. If you study the games of professionals (See Chapter 13), you'll notice that they'll alternate between shots to the right and to the left, between deep (long) and short balls. They frequently vary services, change the speed of their service returns, and utilize every type of stroke. Experienced tournament experts of all ages can chase and surprise a weaker person so much that he (or she) never knows what happens until the final score. Other strategists have learned to set up a pattern and then break it. All the while, they're light and bouncy on their feet, conserving energy while the other person gets physically exhausted.

Effective singles players do not just return a ball; instead, nearly all their shots pack a *purpose.* Each placement depends on the opponent's soft spots and location.

Billie Jean King, one of America's finest tennis strategists at work. *Photo by Art Seitz.*

An interested singles player learns much by challenging many different people. This is not as impossible as it may seem: most municipal American parks are full of individuals who want to play against someone new. At some city courts you usually can find a person who came alone and seeks a partner; it also is proper to ask a couple of players if you can take on the winner.

Gladys Heldman, publisher of *World Tennis,* puts it this way:

> Play against a variety of games—against spin artists, touch players, sluggers, retrievers, tacticians, strokeless wonders. Each type of opponent provides a different challenge. You can develop an assortment of ripostes against chop artists, big servers, net-rushers, dinkers, lefties and players with big forehands or undercut backhands or heavy topspins.

A recreational player would do well to challenge someone *better* on occasion, even at the risk of defeat. Self-confidence is worth its weight in points, of course.

John Gardiner, who supervises tennis instruction of vacationers at his resorts, compiled some valuable tips for winning match points:

1. Analyze your opponent. Does he move well laterally, up and back? Does he like speed or slow shots? Does he stop when rushing net? Is he a slow starter? (Do not let him get a chance to warm up.) If you have played him before, is his best shot working? If not, attack it. Does he get impatient in long rallies?

2. Try to figure out early what your opponent's weaknesses are so he does not get a chance to find out yours.

3. Try to put your opponent on the defense right away with deep, consistent serves to his weakness; this keeps him from attacking behind his returns.

4. Get an early advantage by trying your best early in the match. If you get ahead first you may never be behind again.

5. Play it safe and play percentages. Do not always try the hardest shot in order to get applause.

6. On return of serve send high, deep shots to an opponent's backhand. You have taken the bite out of his big serve by forcing him to move back from the base line.

7. When in bad position against a net man, lob or hit cross court. Cross courts keep him from angling the ball away from you.

8. Be flexible and able to change tactics if you are losing.

9. Do not ease up; keep up the will to win! A winner never quits. Always win the last point.

# CHAPTER 8

*Photo courtesy Bermuda News Bureau.*

# Playing Doubles

There are sound reasons why so many Americans are attracted to the doubles scene. With the help of a partner, one needs to cover less court. There is less running and less exhaustion. Moreover, doubles encourages an interesting combination of participants. Two men can play against two men and two women against two women; or a man and a woman against the same ("mixed doubles"). Some tournaments feature father-and-son combinations or mothers and daughters challenging more mothers and daughters. In country clubs and tennis clubs, a doubles game is considered a pleasant way of socializing, finding potential dates, meeting other married couples, or getting acquainted with other businessmen.

Like golf, doubles tennis is a good mixer, adding a "togetherness" quality to a sport, where also you can be alone. Lastly, there is the matter of money. Playing doubles costs less. At elegant resorts or expensive indoor courts, a foursome pays only half as much as two singles. The hourly court rental rate is split by the two teams, and you save on tennis balls.

Doubles offers a strong appeal to women; the game is fast rather than muscle wrenching. Experienced older persons find doubles enjoyable, because they can use their volleys and lobs, and angle shots and chops, instead of powerhouse ground strokes. A doubles player may not hit the ball as often, but the rallies are usually longer, with more action and a chance to keep going for longer periods without strain. On the other hand, doubles demands a special expertise and alertness. A neophyte may be lost on a court with three aggressive people. The action is too swift, with too much net-rushing, tricky half volleys, drop shots, at-your-feet-shots, unreturnable smashes, and most of all, volleyed exchanges. Besides, anyone will at first struggle with the subtleties of doubles teamwork.

Many singles players prefer to battle it out against only one adversary. They get much more exercise that way. National tennis coaches insist that the doubles play won't do much for your singles competitions, and some advanced players therefore shun the doubles courts. Some individuals like to play on their own because they don't want to rely on someone else. A few top-class singles are loners at heart and they have no intention of sharing the court with a partner.

The partnership is not always easy. Ideally four people should be approximately matched in ability or they won't have much fun. Like other relationships, doubles tennis often depends on consideration, tact, harmony, and a liking for the other person. A team loses its strength if one member tries to grab all the balls or all the credit, or worse, if one individual pushes the other around. Manners go a long way: each duo must avoid open criticism or a display of annoyance or anger. At least outwardly, the team is always unified and at peace with one another.

If one person is the better player—and his partner is willing to listen—some advice may be helpful. But such coaching or any constructive criticizing should take place behind the scenes and out of earshot from the opposing players. One coach observed a fellow who was "glaring, growling, exhorting and spurring his partner ever onward." Good teamwork extends to tactics.

The partners should talk strategy ahead of time. They decide who serves from what side, who protects the middle, who takes which shots. Contrary to what some people believe, a doubles partner *can* cover a larger part of the court. This is especially the case when you're teamed with a slower or newer player.

The intrusion into the teammate's territory is called "poaching." Unsuccessful poaching—or ball stealing—opens up your side of the court to the two rivals. Unplanned poaching among new players can add a note of confusion to the game.

Here are some common reasons for poaching:

1. If you have more know-how with that particular shot
2. If you're in a better location to take the ball

"Poaching," i.e., taking your partner's ball, is allowed and occasionally encouraged in doubles. *Photo by Bob McIntyre.*

3. If your partner is off balance

4. If you're able to "put it away" and gain a quick knockout point

5. As a tactic and learning experience. (Unless you poach occasionally, the other doubles players will think you're not alive.)

The teamwork in these situations includes proper signals, at least for beginning or intermediate doubles players. Some teams may agree on a hand signal beforehand; or they'll simply call out, "I'll take it!" or "Please cross!" or "Mine!" or "Yours!" or "Go ahead!"

Top tournament teams have often worked together so much and for so long that they can anticipate a partner's move with accuracy, so that both people do the right thing. They cross at will, like the hands of a concert pianist, and they no longer need signals. Their court travel resembles that of Siamese twins, with a few yards between them.

Both the pace and the strategy of a doubles game differ from singles in a number of ways. Some of the difference has to do with the additional nine-foot width of the doubles court and with one team member almost always being near the net. In doubles, the base-line-to-base-line power play is reduced: you're either in the back court or at the net; the rest of the terrain is considered "no man's land," where a doubles expert has no business to be. If you stand in "no man's land" (midcourt), one of your opponents can fire at your feet. The ideal exchange of shots should be low, forcing the other team to hit up.

Much of a doubles game takes place in the service courts. To be sure, many coaches consider the serve the most important shot in doubles. If the opposition cannot return your serve, they cannot possibly win. Considering that a big time chunk in tennis consists of serves, one should develop a reliable first delivery that goes in at least 70 percent of the time. Try to have two fairly identical services in doubles, in place of the hard first service and a soft second one.

The serving team has a distinct offensive advantage over the receivers; they can gain an early lead by having the stronger person serve first. Here are the standard positions:

1.    The doubles server should stand behind the base line about five feet from the center stripe, or midway between the center and the sideline (unlike the singles player, who serves from near the center). One of the classic doubles serves is directed into the opponent's backhand corner. This type of shot can be made easily from near the singles sideline.

2.    Another favorite serve is aimed at the center of a service court. Your partner's location is behind the net, but no closer than six feet. He is most effective as a volleyer if he keeps to about the center of the service court, as measured from the outer border of the alley.

Doubles play is more social and less strenuous than singles. *Photo courtesy Palm Springs Convention and Visitors Bureau.*

The receiver meanwhile waits near the singles line. His position may be adjusted according to the service pattern. The harder the service, the more he should stand back, of course. Weak backhand players should be receiving in the forehand courts. The receiver's partner stands in the center some eight to ten feet behind the net.

As the game is launched, each player has a distinct role. Here is how one doubles strategist delineates it:

1.  The server aims for the receiver's backhand and rushes the net to the middle of the service court on the right side.

2.  The receiver attempts to keep the ball away from the server's partner at the net. The receiver aims for the feet of the onrushing server.

3.  If the receiver hits at the server's feet, the receiver's partner rushes into the net to volley any half-volley efforts of the server.

4.  If the receiver hits a weak service return for an easy volley by either side, the partner of the receiver runs back to the base line.

5.  Normally, the serving team drives the two opponents back to the base line. If the two now successfully hit through the middle or around the net players, they will win the point quickly. However, it is usually safer to lob over the net men.

6.  To cope with lobs, the net team retreats a few steps. The player closest to the lob now smashes it.

Net play, the hallmark of doubles, is tricky, and some players must first get accustomed to it. When they do, it will help their singles game as well. (In doubles, 60 to 80 percent of the points are won at the net.) Experienced net players don't just stand there. They present a threat; they keep on the move.

A receiver's partner tries to protect the middle and to volley aggressively in either direction. Good net players try to aim low; they hit as closely as possible to the other's body, so that the player won't have room to move. (Such placements are never meant to be direct body hits to cause injury!) Other volleys are banged into vacant areas between two partners. The net players can cope with returns in form of offensive lobs by taking a few backward steps, and use overheads, if feasible.

At tennis clinics, instructors always stress that the return of serve is crucial in the doubles game. The receiver should get the ball back at all costs, and not attempt to put it away. Instructors can tell you why. By just returning the ball safely, a player decreases the number of his errors while increasing the chance of the opposition's errors. One doubles expert gives another compelling reason. "There will be tremendous pressure on the server when he knows, or rather believes, that he has to play another shot to win the point."

Doubles players in action. Note positions of players. *Photo courtesy Bermuda News Bureau.*

Experienced doubles players like to return the ball cross court; they can hit a larger area this way, besides clearing the net, which is lower in the middle. A well-paced cross-court return allows the server to race toward the net. His partner is already there, and the first team there can take command of the whole court. If the other two players respond in kind, there may be swift and exciting net exchanges. In some international tournaments, the ball won't touch the court for long volleyed rallies.

Experienced players learn to vary their returns to keep the others guessing. Some skillful receivers chop the ball, which flies high and lands on an undefended spot.

Good doubles teams coordinate their tactics, to set up shots for one another or to crisscross into each other's area as gracefully as two ballet dancers.

# PART FOUR

## Tennis Know-How for All

The glittering Acapulco Princess boasts a number of indoor courts with expensive surfaces. *Photo courtesy Acapulco Princess Hotel.*

# CHAPTER 9

# Courts and Surfaces

The playing characteristics of various court surfaces vary greatly, and the player must adapt himself to a variety of ball bounces.

Different court materials have their own idiosyncrasies and their special effect on a customer's legs, which may fatigue more easily. Professional competitors face a special dilemna: their livelihood depends on analyzing a court as quickly as possible. On their travels, the champions must play on new type of surfaces; they may perform one weekend on certain synthetic fibers or bonded layers of plastics; a few days later, with one difficult tournament behind them, touring pros find themselves forced to re-hone their strokes and redesign their footwork for ultra-fast wood floors, or for the high ricochet of clay, or for the speed on hard courts.

Each kind of tennis facility makes its own particular demand. Recreational players will find it useful to know what distinguishes one type of court from another.

*Hard surfaces* are common all over the western United States and Canada, with concrete or asphalt being readily available in even our smallest towns. Hard courts can be built at a reasonable cost to serve the public in municipal parks or schools, in tennis clubs, or as adjuncts to hotels and motels. These courts require almost no upkeep, and they're usable even after a blizzard. (At one Denver, Colorado, outdoor club, for instance, you can play almost immediately after the snow is brushed off.) Asphalt and concrete provide an excellent, reliable, and fast bounce. Aggressive tennis aficionados welcome their chance to serve powerfully and rush the net for volleying. On the debit side, concrete is tough on your feet, and you'll tire quickly unless you wear top-quality tennis shoes. And concrete can crack.

The better clubs prefer a slightly more costly hard court, which softens slightly in the sun and is easier on the legs. For these composition courts, the asphalt may be blended with rubber, plastics, or other elements. The asphalt base will be topped by a layer of paint. These hard courts demand little upkeep except hosing and occasional sweeping. (Hard courts should be kept clean, because dirt and dust wear out racket strings and shoes.)

The material dries fast after a rain, and yet does not become unbearably hot under a tropical sky. Such green tennis oases present a pretty picture to the eye, and the painted lines last for a long time. The bounce is generally perfect and predictable.

*Clay courts* have been a tradition in the warm climates of Florida and California, not to mention the rest of the South, the Southwest, and Europe. Clay is cooler than concrete or composition material. At least initially, clay courts demand a smaller investment. The daily upkeep—grading, sprinkling, line-chalking, and rolling—makes costs rise later, though. On outdoor courts, clay surfaces delight players, because of the shock-absorbing qualities. On the other hand, if the sun shines, outdoor clay courts can get dusty. They become useless after a snowstorm and muddy after heavy rains. (Slippery footing.) Clay drains and dries slowly, and caretakers must cope with holes and fissures caused by the moisture. If there should be no maintenance, balls will fly in the strangest ways, making each game a surprise. (The alternative to clay is

Indoor bubbles now allow tennis all year. The surfaces are long-lasting. *Photo by Bob McIntyre.*

Clay courts are excellent for older or slower players. Clay delays the ball, allowing more time for each strike. *Photo courtesy Bermuda News Bureau.*

a special crushed-granular surface, which has better draining qualities and soon becomes playable again.)

Clay is popular around the world. The courts make for extremely high bounces: the ball seems to hover in midair, bringing success to even a first-timer's forehand. The slow pace gives a beginner some extra seconds to get ready. An average player can "slide" into the ball on a clay court, and the extra time makes tennis pleasant indeed. Even competitors can do things that would be impossible on the fast hard courts. The rallies last long enough to please the seniors, and powerful serves are tempered by this surface's softness. If you learn to play on clay, you'll get used to long, comfortable backswings and to leisurely stroke production. Such coddling may have an adverse effect on future competitors.

*Grass* served the originators of the game, who first utilized the green lawns of England, Bermuda, and the U.S. East. A few grass courts still survive at Wimbledon, and are kept up for the sake of some international tournaments. You can view grass courts in America's older tennis clubs—the Philadelphia Cricket Club is one example—but the officers and managers are plagued by big maintenance expenses. Grass must be seeded and reseeded, fertilized, cropped, and endlessly watered. At one point, the Forest Hills, New York, grass courts required an army of gardeners.

The turf is marvelous on your feet, however. You can run as much as you wish without getting too exhausted, and the green is soothing to the eyes. Nature's own product—grass!—is infinitely prettier than synthetics. Besides, grass is luxuriously cool and pleasant. The characteristic bounce is a low one, and you must get there fast to retrieve the ball.

Tournament competitors criticize the turf for its erratic, eccentric qualities. The bounces *are* sometimes tricky, and the ball may skip and do other capricious things. A lawn becomes slick in the rain, and your tennis shoes make squishing sounds. (Spikes are worn in major grass tournaments.) Top tournament players would prefer that all grass courts be converted to more reliable and less-seasonal surfaces.

*Synthetics* may fulfill some of these needs. The assorted plastics or synthetic carpet fibers are mostly for indoor purposes, although you occasionally see them outdoors, too. Durability can be planned at the factory level by

Grass is pleasant on a player's legs although hard to maintain. *Photo courtesy British Tourist Authority.*

means of quality control. Synthetics always served competitors in the shape of portable courts that may be carted from one arena and auditorium to the next. Synthetics are the be-all and end-all of most plush indoor courts.

Unfortunately, there is one major problem with these products: The price is too high. Certain wonder surfaces cannot be installed for less than $10,000. A sum of $15,000 to $20,000 often buys only the top layers; the graded base, the padding and filling drive up the expenditure still further. Acrylic fibers and the plastics are actually out of the price range of most individuals who want to build their private courts, and only the wealthiest people can afford the many available miracle surfaces. Some of the latter may be bonded to fast-playing wood for indoor courts or asphalt, to various rubberized or foam layers, or to cork and other components.

Indoor courts with artificial fiber surfaces are now popular. *Photo courtesy American Gas Association.*

Synthetic courts vary enormously, cushioning your steps or causing severe leg pains (especially if you play for hours, as instructors must do). Veteran resident pros resist the installation of expensive, unproven materials. A well-known California head pro, who acts as a consultant to investors and directs construction at some western resorts, speaks for some of his peers when he says, "Synthetics are not economical. You can build indoor or outdoor courts without overspending." The colorful names of the inventions do not impress international competitors. After playing for many years on various artificial surfaces, one world-championship pro warns that some of the best-known brands produce too high a bounce. He claims that the synthetic carpets "exaggerate the use of spin. The ball seems to continue on its path as if drawn by an unseen magnet."

# CHAPTER 10

Sweaters can be a good idea on cold days. *Photo by Art Coleman.*

# Tennis Medicine

Tennis appeals to so many Americans of all ages because it is a "no risk" sport. Serious injuries are rare and the dangers found in sky diving, ski racing, and rock climbing do not exist on tennis courts. A tennis player seldom suffers a fracture. In fact, one encounters many white-haired men and women who devoted a lifetime to this sport without suffering a sprain. Despite a strenuous career, most touring pros never get hurt enough for hospitalization. Tennis isn't football.

On the other hand, weekend enthusiasts often end up with elbow inflammations, shoulder pains, or pulled leg muscles. None of the above afflictions are fatal, and they can be avoided. Orthopedic surgeons point out that if you keep fit, you are less likely to incur muscle injuries. Some basic calisthenics, such as those described in Chapter 1, are recommended; in addition, doctors

119

suggest a long-range exercise program with weights. Specialists at the George-town University Medical Center, in Washington, D. C., claim that such work-outs, if increased gradually, do much for *preventing* accidents, and for helping persons who need physical rehabilitation. Here are some specific exercises:

* *The pendulum arm stretch* improves arm flexibility. Bend at the waist to 90 degrees. Swing a five-pound weight across the front of body to an overhead position. Thirty repetitions. (A pendulum can be combined with windmilling motions of your arms.)

* *The side-and-front arm lift* strengthens muscles of the shoulder blades, front chest, triceps, biceps, and forearm (wrist). Stand erect. Lift the arm to horizontal first in front (hold for five seconds); then move to the side (hold for five seconds); drop slowly to the side. Repeat thirty times. Start with a two-pound weight,—progress to a maximum five-pound weight (women), ten-pound weight (men).

* *The isometric forearm-extensor exercise* adds strength to forearms. Hold the arm extended close to horizontal in front of the body. Actively pull fingers and wrist into fully extended position (hold for five seconds). Pro-gress to fifty repetitions.

Accident prevention begins prior to court time. Experienced profession-als insist, for instance, that *you must warm up before playing tennis.* A Michigan tennis clinic encourages its students to jog (or run) a mile before breakfast. This warm-up period is followed by brief, easy gymnastics, and *then* tennis. The pro at the Palm Springs, California, Tennis Club persuades its members to do a few kneebends and other muscle-stretching movements as they walk to the courts. (*Deep* kneebends can subject the knee to cartilage damage; half kneebends are, therefore, better.) Even beginners would do well to rub their muscles for a few minutes or pump their arms up and down for increased circulation. Dr. Arnold Heller, a well-known Colorado bone specialist, agrees that cold tissues are in greater danger to sustain injuries than warm ones.

A chilly outside temperature dictates that you wear a sweater or a warm-up suit when you hit the first balls. As you get hot, you may discard the garments, which can be put on again after a set. Start off with gentle strokes;

increase the intensity bit by bit. Never serve hard when you're still cold. Too much power can tear the muscle fibers in your arm or shoulder. Older players should be especially careful not to start off with cannonball serves. Make a few shadow motions, or windmill gyrations, and then serve lightly. Bill Smith, a respected resident pro on the west coast puts it this way:

> No successful $100,000-per-year baseball pitcher would think of pitching a game without vigorously massaging his elbow and arm. This draws blood to the area and thereby "splints" and protects the arm during play. Pitchers would be reprimanded by their managers if they neglected to cover their pitching arm between innings or afterward. Pitchers *never* start out without gradual warm-up tosses before throwing the "big one."

After a long stint on the courts, it is wise to keep out of drafty or super-air-conditioned rooms. Put on a sweater to hold onto the warmth and to protect your body.

You're more liable to suffer from muscle injuries and inflammations by playing for too long a period, using too much force, or stroking incorrectly. There is also a greater chance to get hurt if you're exhausted and insist on "just one more game."

The most frequent complaint concerns an ailment that goes under the broad label "tennis elbow." The pain can range from a light, occasional throbbing to severe agony. Some victims cry out if they must lift a cup of coffee; others can no longer extend their forearm. The worst sufferers find it difficult to turn a doorknob, or worse, they can no longer carry out occupations that depend on arms. (The malady also attacks carpenters, among several other professions.)

Tennis elbow involves: (a) inflammation or (b) tears of tissues, or both. Aging players will be more apt to develop this condition, and a few unlucky individuals are saddled with it on a *chronic* basis. For some people, the pain disappears after some rest.

Tennis-elbow patients will be helped by strengthening exercises *and by learning the proper stroke techniques.*

Dr. Robert Nirschl, an Arlington, Virginia, orthopedic surgeon and one

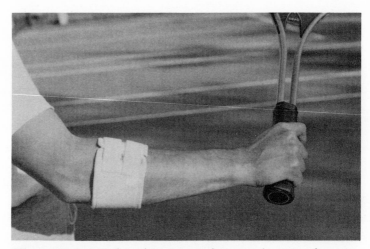

Elbow supports such as this one can decrease the pain of tennis elbow. *Photo courtesy Dr. R. P. Nirschl.*

of America's leading researchers in this field, states that faulty backhands must be corrected. According to Dr. Nirschl, some players use their forearms as the sole power source. This strains the elbow, of course. In discussing the backhand with pros, Dr. Nirschl has come up with these specific suggestions:

1.  Keep the front shoulder down, with the trunk leaning toward net.
2.  Keep the elbow and wrist as firm as possible.
3.  Hit the ball in front of you.
4.  Let the power come from your shoulder muscles and by means of body-weight transfer, not from your forearm.
5.  Avoid extreme wrist roll.

Physicians and pros agree that a correct racket size is important. Too large or too small a racket grip can result eventually in tennis elbow. If the handle is too big and the racket too heavy, an inflammation will be aggravated. Sometimes a size can be decreased by as little as one-eighth. Also, the racket should not be strung too tightly. If you're prone to tennis elbow, a 50- to 55-lb. string job suffices. The more softly a tennis racket is strung, the less strain; and the more flexible the material—like natural lamb gut instead of nylon—the better.

There are still some mysteries: Why do sufferers experience the sudden disappearance of pain after switching to a different racket? Wood or metal? Doctors do not share the same opinions, but a majority consulted for this book recommended that a player change to a flexible, lighter, *wood* racket. One authority on sports injuries explains why: "Wood dampens the indirect stress of a tennis ball on the elbow." It seems that stiff metal transmits this force and intensifies the impact. "A very rigid metal racket should be a 'no-no' for the average patient," counsels Dr. Arnold Heller, who is himself a player.

The medical profession sometimes recommends the use of a wide elastic support band around the forearm. Such a brace absorbs and redistributes some of the force, and eases the stress on the muscle ligaments in the area. The band should be kept fairly tight.

Depending on the severity, a player can often find relief with a few aspirin tablets before a game. Heat pads and warm compresses prove their worth prior to court time. A sauna works for people with healthy hearts and little desire to compete. (A sauna warms your tissues but also makes you tired.)

The use of ice bags after a game has merit. In cases of severe pain, the ice should be kept on for several hours.

If none of these simple things help, physicians will try other remedies. Among them are the following:

*Ultrasound treatments administered by physical therapists

*Radiation in small doses under the supervision of a doctor specializing in radiology

*Cortisone shots for acute cases (can be painful)

*Surgery as a last resort for chronic conditions (after two years or longer)

The above measures also apply to shoulder and knee injuries, and to the pulling of the plantar muscle. In the latter case, the symptom is a sudden sharp pain in the calf, as though hit by a bullet, which will cause a temporary limp. Orthopedic surgeons keep the afflicted off their feet, and supply crutches for locomotion. The lack of a previous warm-up period, old age, or insufficient physical conditioning all increase the possibilities of these medical problems.

Common sense and caution are important. Always remove all balls from the playing area! Some people have fallen over balls and sprained their ankles.

Sprains can be treated with an ice pack. If the limb does not get better, see a doctor, who may prescribe pain pills and furnish you with elastic bandages. These are available in two-, three-, and four-inch widths from drugstores.

Elastic bandages give comfort and support to ligament, tendon, and muscle sprains and strains. Dr. Nirschl offers two warnings, however:

Dr. R. P. Nirschl, a leading expert in tennis injuries, with patient. *Photo courtesy Dr. R. P. Nirschl.*

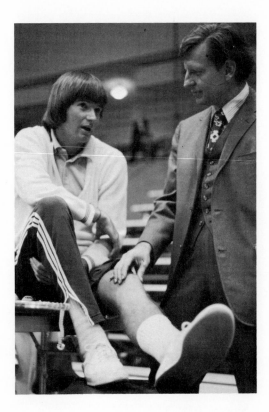

One: Sprains result from ligament stretch and tears when joints are forced into exaggerated positions. An elastic bandage cannot be depended upon to prevent a recurrence, because of its flexible support nature.

Two: Application of elastic bandages, especially on knees and elbows can cause blockage of blood circulation, and can result in swelling.

If you need firm support of joints for athletic activities, you should consider nonelastic straps or taping.

Some people ignore symptoms of sprains or tears and won't bother to seek medical attention, despite their suspicion of an injury. Others are fool-hardy enough to refuse first aid. Professional tournament players, although usually in excellent physical condition, show a tendency to abuse their muscles until damage is severe. An operation, then, remains the only solution. Some of the most-famous tennis names have ignored pain. As a result, they found themselves out of action for weeks or even months.

Billie Jean King and Rod Laver, among others, have suffered from aggravated injuries. A few champions actually had to drop out of competition forever.

Tennis courts are not ski slopes, but they can be occasional traps for an assortment of mishaps and emergencies. First-aid knowledge proves useful in the case of a bad fall and sprawl, sunstroke, or overexertion and cardiac troubles. Some persons show little judgment, such as the player who won a city championship. He exuberantly jumped over the net and fell on his face, breaking several teeth and gashing his chin badly. A seventy-year old oil executive risked his life by indulging in game after game at a 6,000-foot elevation. The heat was too much, and he fainted after the fourth set. When his doctor recommended that he cut down, the old man laughed in his face. He eventually died of a heart attack on the courts.

## FIRST-AID ON THE COURT

All tennis players should know how to handle certain medical emergencies. Here are some simple pointers:

## Fainting

The victim loses consciousness. Although still breathing, the patient is noticeably pale, the pallor caused by a reduced blood supply to the brain. The fainted person should be made to stretch out in a cool place, head lower than the legs. Loosen the player's clothing. A little water in the face will have a reviving effect. Give smelling salts, if available.

## Heart attack

When heart seizure is suspected, do not alarm the player, but reassure him. Symptoms: pale face, white lips, breathing difficulty, intense pain in chest, shoulder, and arm, and extreme anxiety. Place the patient in a reclining position and keep him comfortable by loosening his shirt buttons. If conscious, give him coffee or tea. Call the doctor at once. Do not transport the person or make him walk; wait for an ambulance. Give mouth-to-mouth rescuscitation if breathing stops. If heart stops beating, give external cardiac massage and interrupt it every thirty seconds to fill chest two or three times by mouth-to-mouth resuscitation in case a second person is not available.

## Bleeding

Minor bleeding usually can be controlled by pressure on the wound with a sterile dressing or freshly laundered cloth. Severe bleeding may require the use of a tourniquet. Do not apply the latter unless all other methods fail and the victim's life appears endangered. It is possible for the patient to go into shock when a tourniquet is removed. Let the doctor handle this. Internal bleeding always requires a physician's attention.

## Problems Caused by Sun and Heat

Long hours on a tennis court in a hot climate can result in heat exhaustion, indicated by a white face, a clammy skin, and exhaustion. Doctors suggest that a player gets off the court for some rest and liquids. Heat stroke is more serious. It can be prevented by drinking enough water or juices, an appropriate head cover, the possible use of salt tablets, and sponging with moist cloths. Severe instances of heat stroke can be recognized by fainting, dizziness, nausea, and vomiting; in all cases, there is an elevated temperature and a rapid pulse. Help the victim into the shade or a cool room. Elevate the head and apply cold compresses to it. If he is conscious, make him drink and take salt tablets. Otherwise, call for medical attention.

Competition playing requires intake of sufficient liquids. *Photo by Curtis Casewit.*

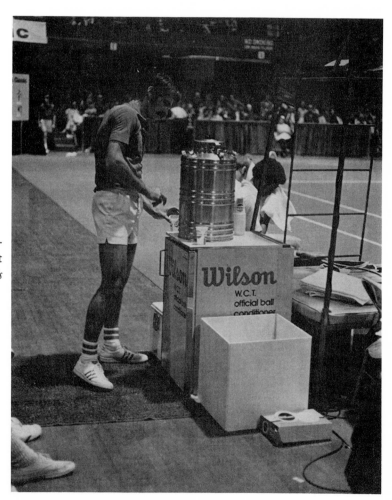

If you hit the ball frequently, you'll also profit from information about a correct diet. Tournament players realize the importance of not eating a big meal just before a match; at least two or three hours should elapse for digestion, which must not interfere while you're on the court. Before a taxing tennis session, take a salt tablet; it will prevent cramps later on. (Cramps can be caused by the loss of salt in your body.) Salt tablets are regularly given to the tennis students in southwestern tennis ranches.

Some coaches make it a point to warn against taking extra sugar, dextrose, or honey before competing. This gives you a high rise in blood-sugar level, which sets off an increased flow of body insulin. The lowering of your blood sugar to below normal can result in a sudden feeling of tiredness. You may undo a week of training in five minutes.

During a match, you can refresh yourself with water, Gatorade, and other noncarbonated drinks. Orange slices are excellent. Long hours of tennis playing will increase your need for the replacement of liquids. According to one celebrated player, the night after a match calls for an adult competitor to "drink plenty of beer. If you won, make it champagne!"

# CHAPTER 11

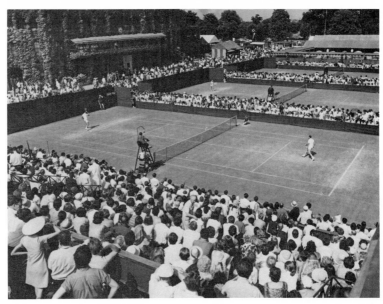

All competitors dream of Wimbledon. *Photo courtesy British Tourist Authority.*

# Tennis Etiquette

No matter how forcefully a player may smash an overhead, he will find himself in a weak position if he ignores the rules of tennis etiquette. The protocol of the sport began on British and then on American lawns. The players were well-bred; they acted accordingly. The old English stiffness is long gone, but fair play and sportsmanship remain.

Modern tennis etiquette has its practical reasons: if we want to be treated with consideration by others, we must reciprocate in kind. Good manners are important currency within the confines of tennis clubs, of country clubs, and in our more distinguished resort hotels. Major matches require a decorum that is adopted also by recreational players in many places.

Tennis etiquette starts with appropriate attire. What's appropriate? It depends on where you chose to play. Pastel colors and off-whites are consid-

129

Rosemary Casals.

ered correct on many courts. Women's tennis dresses may come with some adornments.

The story is different for men. Novelty shirts or shirts with flowers are unacceptable except on some public courts. A fellow makes a poor impression if he appears in a T-shirt and in cut-off jeans. Both are taboo in clubs or clinics. It is not a good idea to wear track shorts, striped Bermuda shorts, or long slacks. Tennis shoes—not basketball shoes or street shoes—are a must even on city-owned installations. At various tennis schools, tennis "colleges," or tennis "ranches," a student is expected to pick a different shirt color from that of his instructor, mostly to avoid confusion.

Few resort hotels insist on all white, but garments should be fresh and clean. One California tennis vacation mecca will refuse entry to anyone in a dirty shirt or in dirty tennis shoes. "If you dress nicer, you act nicer," goes one club's slogan. At some clubs, white is still right. On cold mornings gym suits are acceptable for both men and women. Except for games in steaming climates on city courts, men cannot take off their tennis shirts. Bare, hairy chests are taboo on better courts, including those owned by condominium and apartment complexes.

A player must be familiar with the rules of tennis. He should know the various lines that demarcate fore courts and back courts and service boxes. The ability to keep accurate score is taken for granted. Obviously, both players must get a chance to warm up before starting a game. A person cannot begin until the other is ready, which need not take an inordinate time. In the same vein, each singles player is entitled to try a few serves without point-counting. The warm-up procedure should exclude an immediate barrage of cannonball serves, or the temptation to chase an opponent from one corner to the other.

A player may possess the world's best volley but the world's worst competition manners, such as laughing after gaining a point or cussing after losing one. Praise should be given sparingly; too much talk is offensive, and even acquaintances resent stroke or strategy critique unless they ask for it. It is frowned upon to coach someone or to show condescension toward a weaker person or complain about the techniques of a strong one. Etiquette demands that we never argue with an opponent, or worse, with an official.

Most matches take place without the benefit of linesmen and umpires. It is, therefore, easy enough to cheat in a game; after all, a player is expected to call the balls on his side. "Tennis reveals your character," Bill Smith, a California pro, tells his students. "An honest man on a tennis court is surely an honest man in business, too." Cheating is thus a cardinal sin; good sportsmanship implies that a dubious point should be decided in favor of the other person. If in doubt, a point can also be replayed.

John Gardiner, known for creating the first tennis-vacation clinics many decades ago, always encouraged his students to compete against one another.

These matches take place after several hours of instruction.

Gardiner sends each person into "combat" with these reminders:

1.  Avoid quick serving. Wait till your opponent is ready, state the score, and then serve. If someone is rushing you, raise your hand and signal "not ready."

2.  Keep track of the score. It is the responsibility of the server to call the score before each point.

3.  When making a call do not ask a spectator for his opinion, because (a) it may annoy your opponent; (b) the spectator may not be in a position to see it; (c) he may be prejudiced; and (d) he may be unqualified.

4.  Try to make instantaneous calls. If, for example, on a fast serve where the ball may be back in play or in the net before a call can be made, the receiver's shot must be considered an attempted play. If the server thought it was out, he must play the return anyway or he loses the point.

5.  Any ball that cannot be called out is good, and a player cannot call a "let" if he did not see it.

6.  In doubles, if one player calls a ball out and the other calls it good, play the ball as good.

7.  Returning bad serves often upsets the momentum of the server. Try blocking them into the net or letting them go back to the fence.

8.  Any conversation between partners or among all players during a point is distracting, with the exception of "out," "in," "switch," etc.

Gardiner concludes: "Tennis is a game of great customs and traditions which are not found in the rule book. Not only should one know the rules but good manners are essential to your game."

There also exists an unwritten code suited to each occasion. If a player loses points, for instance, he need not come up with excuses that his equipment is at fault or that he had the flu last week. In clubs, members are considered discourteous who refuse to play an equal or who deny a lesser player the chance to rally for a few moments.

A truly great competitor shows his mettle when he is pitted, not against the strongest man, but against one of the gentlest. Will the super athlete keep up his relentless fire of services and returns? Is it necessary to make tennis war on a weak opponent with countless passing shots, angle volleys, or base-line placements? Must the recognized international champion win his sets with a 6:0, 6:0? Not necessarily. While on a pro tour, Arthur Ashe had to face a local pro whose forte happened to be children's instruction. The pro was a success in his special field; in fact, several hundred youngsters came to watch him "defeat" Arthur Ashe.

Despite his good form and clean strokes, the local hero was no match for someone of Ashe's caliber. Ashe won the first set almost without effort. During the second set, the famous champion began to strike the ball with slightly less pace. He hit volleys that stood a chance of being returned. Ashe's celebrated services steamed a little less, too. Suddenly, the local pro looked

Arthur Ashe. *Photo by Art Seitz.*

good with his young audience. Ashe won handsomely, and he did so in more ways than one.

Some advanced players let the not-so-strong gain an occasional victory, thus taking the sting out of a defeat. After all, the loser can say, he won one game out of six. The civilized champion does not mention his secret, of course, and the reasons for losing those points are never mentioned.

Resort hotels, clubs or teaching centers generally post court rules. At an apartment complex overlooking Lake Tahoe, players must observe an etiquette that applies elsewhere, too:

1.   All courts will be reserved on an hourly basis.

2.   Courts may be reserved one day in advance.

3.   A second court reservation may not be made until the time of the initial reservation has elapsed.

4.   Names of all individuals playing on a court must appear on the reservation sheet. No player's name may appear on more than one reservation. The use of fictitious names, or an intentional effort to circumvent this rule, will cause the reservation of the offenders to be canceled.

5.   You must be at the courts ten minutes before the hour of your reservation. If you are not, the hostess will fill the hour from a waiting list.

6.   The decision of the tennis hostess will be final. All complaints regarding the decision of the court hostess will be directed to the tennis director.

One should arrive punctually and, equally important, give up a court at the prearranged time. Even a tennis hotshot will be quickly hated for hogging the arena. In the same way, you cannot walk through someone else's playing area while a game is in progress. Indeed, it is a sign of courtesy to think of your neighbor. A quarreling couple on one court will offend the couple on the next one. Loud conversations and enthusiastic outpourings cut into someone else's concentration. When retrieving a stray ball on a neighboring court, wait until the point is over before attempting to get it. In returning a stray ball to another court, don't hit the ball anywhere just to get it off your court.

Most good competitors started young. *Photo courtesy Vic Braden Tennis College.*

Pick it up and hit it directly to one of the players. A player is supposed to pick up the balls on his side of the net, and furnish two or three to the server. Some club members irritate others by not picking up their share of balls, by delivering them to the other side with too much force, or by making the other party pluck them out of the court corners. If you are ready for serving, and find yourself out of the fuzzy ammunition, a polite "We're missing some balls" is better than "They're on your side! Get them, and be quick about it!" (It is also a good idea for each person to bring his own supply.)

Tournaments dictate their own set of rules, some of which are unwritten. A long stall before a service rates as questionable behavior, and it is bad form to take overlong breaks between games. No one wants to lose points. But if it happens, it is better to be graceful than angry. Temper tantrums may vent a competitor's feelings; on the other hand, a thrown racket tells something about his personality. Lack of self-control produces little admiration from the audience. Even famous net stars like Billie Jean King and others sometimes kick balls in fury. Pancho Gonzalez once stormed into the tribunes to silence a heckler, and some South Americans are known to hurl equipment. (By contrast, certain players keep their cool even if they're booed during an entire set.) During the professional world championships several players regularly smash balls into the bleachers after losing a point. Not even a million-dollar-a-year income can excuse rudeness on a court.

One final item. Tournament players always shake hands after a match and thank the referee.

Manners maketh the tennis man, and the tennis woman, too.

# CHAPTER 12

# Rules and Scoring

Here is the Official Code of the International Lawn Tennis Federation, of which the United States Lawn Tennis Association is a member:

## THE SINGLES GAME

Rule 1: Dimensions and Equipment

The Court shall be a rectangle, 78 feet long and 27 feet wide. It shall be divided across the middle by a net, suspended from a cord or metal cable of a maximum diameter of one-third of an inch, the ends of which shall be attached to, or pass over, the tops of two posts, 3 feet, 6 inches high, the center of which shall stand 3 feet outside the Court on each side. The height of the net shall be 3 feet at the center, where it shall be held down taut by a strap not more than 2 inches wide. There shall be a band

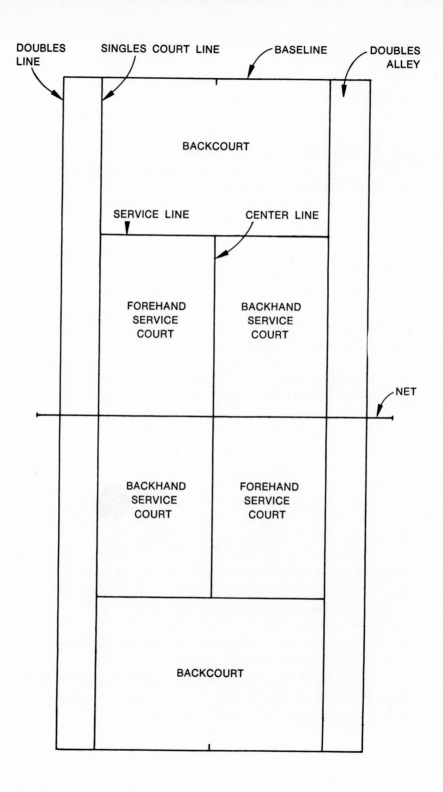

DOUBLES
LINE

SINGLES COURT LINE

BASELINE

DOUBLES
ALLEY

BACKCOURT

SERVICE LINE

CENTER LINE

FOREHAND
SERVICE
COURT

BACKHAND
SERVICE
COURT

NET

BACKHAND
SERVICE
COURT

FOREHAND
SERVICE
COURT

BACKCOURT

covering the cord or metal cable and the top of the net for not less than 2 inches nor more than 2 1/2 inches in depth on each side. The lines bounding the ends and sides of the Court shall respectively be called the Base-lines and the Side-lines. On each side of the net, at a distance of 21 feet from it and parallel with it, shall be drawn the Service-lines. The space on each side of the net between the Service-line and the Side-lines shall be divided into two equal parts called the Service-Courts by the center Service-line, which must be 2 inches in width, drawn half-way between, and parallel with, the Side-lines. Each Base-line shall be bisected by an imaginary continuation of the center Service-line to a line 4 inches in length and 2 inches in width called the center mark drawn inside the Court at right angles to and in contact with such Base-lines. All other lines shall be not less than 1 inch nor more than 2 inches in width, except the Base-line, which may be 4 inches in width, and all measurements shall be made to the outside of the lines.

Rule 2:   Permanent Fixtures

The permanent fixtures of the Court shall include not only the net, posts, cord or metal cable, strap and band, but also, where there are any such, the back and side stops, the stands, fixed or movable seats and chairs round the Court, and their occupants, all other fixtures around and above the Court, and the Umpire, Net cord Judge, Foot fault Judge, Linesmen and Ball Boys when in their respective places.

Rule 3:   Ball—Size, Weight and Bound

The ball shall have a uniform outer surface. If there are any seams they shall be stitchless. The ball shall be more than 2 1/2 inches and less than 2 5/8 inches in diameter, and more than 2 ounces and less than 2 1/16 ounces in weight. The ball shall have a bounce of more than 53 inches and less than 58 inches when dropped 100 inches upon a concrete base.

Rule 4:   Server and Receiver

The players shall stand on opposite sides of the net; the player who first delivers the ball shall be called the Server, and the other the Receiver.

Rule 5:   Choice of Sides and Service

The choice of sides, and the right to be Server or Receiver in the first game, shall be decided by toss. The player winning the toss may choose, or require his opponent to choose:

(a) The right to be Server or Receiver, in which case the other player shall choose the side; or

(b) The side, in which case the other player shall choose the right to be Server or Receiver.

Rule 6:  Delivery of Service

The service shall be delivered in the following manner: Immediately before commencing to serve, the Server shall stand with both feet at rest behind (i.e. farther from the net than) the base line, and within the imaginary continuations of the center-mark and side-line. The server shall then project the ball by hand into the air in any direction and before it hits the ground strike it with his racket, and the delivery shall be deemed to have been completed at the moment of the impact of the racket and the ball. A player with the use of only one arm may utilize his racket for the projection.

Rule 7:  Foot Fault

The server shall throughout the delivery of the service:

(a) Not change his position by walking or running.

(b) Not touch with either foot, any area other than that behind the base line within the imaginary extension of the center mark and side-line.

Rule 8:  From Alternate Courts

(a) In delivering the service, the Server shall stand alternately behind the right and left Courts, beginning from the right in every game. If service from a wrong half of the Court occurs and is undetected, all play resulting from such wrong service or services shall stand, but the inaccuracy of the station shall be corrected immediately it is discovered.

(b) The ball served shall pass over the net and hit the ground within the Service Court which is diagonally opposite, or upon any line bounding such Court, before the Receiver returns it.

Rule 9:  Faults

The Service is a fault:

(a) If the Server commit any breach of Rules 6, 7 or 8;

(b) If he miss the ball in attempting to strike it;

(c) If the ball served touch a permanent fixture (other than the net, strap or band) before it hits the ground.

Rule 10:  Service After a Fault

After a fault (if it be the first fault) the Server shall serve again from behind the same half of the Court from which he served that fault, unless the service was from the wrong half, when, in accordance with Rule 8, the Server shall be entitled to one service only from behind the other half. A fault may not be claimed after the next service has been delivered.

Rule 11:   Receiver Must Be Ready

The Server shall not serve until the Receiver is ready. If the latter attempt to return the service, he shall be deemed ready. If, however, the Receiver signify that he is not ready, he may not claim a fault because the ball does not hit the ground within the limits fixed for the service.

Rule 12:   A Let

In all cases where a "Let" has to be called under the rules, or to provide for an interruption to play, it shall have the following interpretations:

(a)   When called solely in respect of a service, that one service only shall be replayed.

(b)   When called under any other circumstance, the point shall be replayed.

Rule 13:   The Service Is a "Let"

If the ball served touch the net, strap or band, and is otherwise good, or, after touching the net, strap or band, touch the Receiver or anything which he wears or carries before hitting the ground.

Rule 14:   When Receiver Becomes Server

At the end of the first game the Receiver shall become Server, and the Server, Receiver; and so on alternately in all the subsequent games of a match. If a player serve out of turn, the player who ought to have served shall serve as soon as the mistake is discovered, but all points scored before such discovery shall be reckoned. If a game shall have been completed before such discovery, the order of service remains as altered. A fault served before such discovery shall not be reckoned.

Rule 15:   Ball in Play Till Point Decided

A ball is in play from the moment at which it is delivered in service. Unless a fault or a let be called, it remains in play until the point is decided.

Rule 16:   Server Wins Point

The Server wins the point:

(a)   If the ball served, not being a let under Rule 13, touch the

Receiver or anything which he wears or carries, before it hits the ground.

(b)  If the Receiver otherwise loses the point as provided by Rule 18.

Rule 17:   Receiver Wins Point

The Receiver wins the point:

(a)  If the Server serve two consecutive faults;

(b)  If the Server otherwise lose the point as provided by Rule 18.

Rule 18:   Player Loses Point

A player loses the point if:

(a)  He fail, before the ball in play has hit the ground twice consecutively, to return it directly over the net (except as provided in Rule 22 (a) or (c); or

(b)  He return the ball in play so that it hits the ground, a permanent fixture, or other object, outside any of the lines which bound his opponent's Court (except as provided in Rule 22 (a) and (c); or

(c)  He volley the ball and fail to make a good return even when standing outside the Court; or

(d)  He touch or strike the ball in play with his racket more than once in making a stroke; or

(e)  He or his racket (in his hand or otherwise) or anything which he wears or carries touch the net, posts, cord or metal cable, strap or band, or the ground within his opponent's Court at any time while the ball is in play; or

(f)  He volley the ball before it has passed the net; or

(g)  The ball in play touch him or anything that he wears or carries, except his racket in his hand or hands; or

(h)  He throws his racket at and hits the ball.

Rule 19:   Player Hinders Opponent

If the player commits any act either deliberate or involuntary which, in the opinion of the Umpire, hinders his opponent in making a stroke, the Umpire shall in the first case award the point to the opponent, and in the second case order the point to be replayed.

Rule 20:   Ball Falling on Line—Good

A ball falling on a line is regarded as falling in the Court bounded by that line.

Rule 21:   Ball Touching Permanent Fixture

If the ball in play touch a permanent fixture (other than the net, posts, cord or metal cable, strap or band) after it has hit the ground, the player who struck it wins the point; if before it hits the ground his opponent wins the point.

Rule 22:  Good Return

It is a good return:

(a) If the ball touch the net, posts, cord or metal cable, strap or band, provided that it passes over any of them and hits the ground within the Court; or

(b) If the ball, served or returned, hit the ground within the proper Court and rebound or be blown back over the net, and the player whose turn it is to strike reach over the net and play the ball, provided that neither he nor any part of his clothes or racket touch the net posts, cord or metal cable, strap or band or the ground within his opponent's Court, and that the stroke be otherwise good; or

(c) If the ball be returned outside the post, either above or below the level of the top of the net, even though it touch the post, provided that it hits the ground within the proper Court; or

(d) If a player's racket pass over the net after he has returned the ball, provided the ball pass the net before being played and be properly returned; or

(e) If a player succeeded in returning the ball, served or in play, which strikes a ball lying in the Court.

Rule 23:  Interference

In case a player is hindered in making a stroke by anything not within his control except a permanent fixture of the Court, or except as provided for in Rule 19, the point shall be replayed.

Rule 24:  The Game

If a player wins his first point, the score is called 15 for that player; on winning his second point, the score is called 30 for that player; on winning his third point, the score is called 40 for that player, and the fourth point won by a player is scored game for that player except as below:

If both players have won three points, the score is called deuce; and the next point won by a player is called advantage for that player. If the same player wins the next point, he wins the game; if the other player wins the next point the score is again called deuce; and so on, until a player wins the two points immediately following the score at deuce, when the game is scored for that player.

Rule 25:   The Set

A player (or players) who first win six games wins a set; except that he must win by a margin of at least two games over his opponent and where necessary a set shall be extended until his margin be achieved.

Rule 26:   When Players Change Sides

The players shall change sides at the end of the first, third and every subsequent alternate game of each set, and at the end of each set unless the total number of games in such set be even, in which case the change is not made until the end of the first game of the next set.

Rule 27:   Maximum Number of Sets

The maximum number of sets in a match shall be 5, or, where women take part, 3.

Rule 28:   Rules Apply to Both Sexes

Except where otherwise stated, every reference in these Rules to the masculine includes the feminine gender.

Rule 29:   Decisions of Umpire and Referee

In matches were an Umpire is appointed, his decision shall be final; but where a Referee is appointed, an appeal shall lie to him from the decision of an Umpire on a question of law, and in all such cases the decision of the Referee shall be final.

Rule 30:   Play shall be continuous from the first service till the match be concluded; provided that the third set, or when women take part, the second set, either player is entitled to a rest, which shall not exceed 10 minutes.

## THE DOUBLES GAME

Rule 31:

The foregoing Rules shall apply to the Doubles Game except as below.

Rule 32:   Dimensions of Court

For the Doubles Game, the Court shall be 36 feet in width, i.e. 4½ feet wider on each side than the Court for the Singles Game, and those portions of the singles Side-lines which lie between the two Service-lines shall be called the Service-side-lines. In other respects, the Court shall be similar to that described in Rule 1, but the portions of the Singles Side-lines between the base-line and Service-line on each side of the net may be omitted if desired.

Rule 33:   Order of Service

The order of serving shall be decided at the beginning of each set as follows:

The pair who have to serve in the first game of each set shall decide which partner shall do so and the opposing pair shall decide similarly for the second game. The partner of the player who served in the first game shall serve in the third; the partner of the player who served in the second game shall serve in the fourth, and so on in the same order in all the subsequent games of a set.

Rule 34:   Order of Receiving

The order of receiving the service shall be decided at the beginning of each set as follows:

The pair who have to receive the service in the first game shall decide which partner shall receive the first service, and that partner shall continue to receive the first service in every odd game throughout that set. The opposing pair shall likewise decide which partner shall receive the first service in the second game and that partner shall continue to receive the first service in every even game throughout that set. Partners shall receive the service alternately throughout each game.

Rule 35:   Service Out of Turn

If a partner serve out of his turn, the partner who ought to have served shall serve as soon as the mistake is discovered, but all points scored, and any faults served before such discovery, shall be reckoned. If a game shall have been completed before such discovery, the order of service remains as altered.

Rule 36:   Error in Order of Receiving

If during a game the order of receiving the service is changed by the Receivers it shall remain as altered until the end of the game in which the mistake is discovered, but the partners shall resume their original order of receiving in the next game of that set in which they are Receivers of the service.

Rule 37:   Ball Touching Server's Partner Is Fault

The service is a fault as provided for by Rule 9, or if the ball served touch the Server's partner or anything he wears or carries, but if the ball served touch the partner of the Receiver or anything which he wears or carries, not being a let under Rule 13 (a), before it hits the ground, the Server wins the point.

Rule 38:   Ball Struck Alternately

The ball shall be struck alternately by one or other player of the opposing pairs, and if a player touches the ball in play with his racket in contravention of this Rule, his opponents win the point.

"Tie-Breaker":

When a singles game reaches 6/6, many times a "tie-breaker" is used to eliminate prolonged sets, and to keep schedules. A "tie-breaker" can be any agreed upon number of points won first. The 9-point "tie-breaker" is most common in play. Each Server serves 2 points each. The individual or team that hits 5 points first wins. Change sides after 4 points are played. In the event of a 4/4, the last Server serves the final point. Opposing team or player can then decide the side to be served. Players shall stay for one game after a tie-break. The official tie-breaker rules for doubles are patterned according to Singles rules, provided that each player shall serve from the same end of the court in the tie-break game that he has served from during that particular set.

Player A shall serve Points 1 and 2, right court and left court; Player D then serves Points 3 and 4 (R and L); Player B serves Points 5 and 6 (R and L); Player C serves Points 7 and 8 (R and L). (Note that this procedure calls for partners of the second-serving team to serve in reverse sequence.) If the score reaches 4 points all, Player B serves Point 9 from the right or left court at the election of the receiver. The foregoing sequence is followed until 5 points are scored by one of the teams which is then declared the winner of the set.

The professional circuits, including World Championship Tennis, uses a 12-point system. In this case, the tie-breaker is the best of 12 points, providing the winner has a margin of 2. If the score reaches 6-points all, the tie-break game shall continue until one has a 2-point margin.

# PART FIVE

Becoming a Competitor
and Money-Maker

Arthur Ashe.

# CHAPTER 13

# Competition Playing

Not all singles and doubles players are interested in entering tournaments. Indeed, most adults lack time for training, while others, including many older persons, show little inclination to exhaust themselves. Rich Hillway, who grooms young players, estimates that only about 25 percent of his juniors are sufficiently interested in tennis and stick to the sport long enough to become serious competitors. Many who do begin to play at ages eight to twelve.

Arthur Ashe was six when he first showed up to challenge other kids in his home state of Virginia. Rod Laver started at ten. Chris Evert and the Buchholz boys and many of their peers became dedicated to tennis before their teens.

Tennis-playing parents can make a difference. Julie Heldman seems one

Pancho Gonzales. *Photo by Art Seitz.*

good example. Her mother, a former competitor, became the founder and editor of a tennis magazine. Julius Heldman was a national junior champion who later competed as a veteran.

Some players do not come from tennis families, but their parents' lack of interest (or lack of money) need not be detrimental. In the same way, ambitious young people have overcome the obstacles of color or ethnic backgrounds. This was proven by Arthur Ashe, Pancho Gonzales (whose mother gave him his first 57-cent racket), Pancho Segura, and Rosie Casals, among others. Roy Emerson was an Australian farm boy who milked cows, became a track and field winner, and was finally discovered by a tennis coach. Gardnar

Mulloy, a Florida tennis star who helped many juniors, describes the route
of a typical young American.

> Around the age of ten he picks up a tennis racquet and begins to
> fumble his way around the public courts. He discovers a liking and apti-
> tude for the game and devotes more and more of his leisure time to it.
> Soon he is beating all the kids of his own age in the neighborhood and
> many a great deal older. When he is thirteen a local coach is tipped off
> about him, takes a look at the boy, sees latent talent in him and takes him
> in hand. From this moment the lad is taught two things—tennis and the
> will to win. The two things are made to become inseparable in his mind.
> Three years later the boy is winning junior tennis championships.

Here are fifteen ways in which an enthusiastic youngster can speed up
the learning process:

1. Taking part in junior tennis clinics. Many are free. One example:
The National Junior Tennis League, which provides gratis lessons and, in
some areas, equipment. The league has no restrictions as to "race, color,
sex, creed, or nationality." Some free clinics get the benefit of well-known
pros operating in major U.S. cities. The NJTL encourages competition
even for beginners.

2. Joining a tennis club where instruction is available.

3. Attending tennis camps in summer. Several weeks of daily instruction should have some effect, especially on young beginners and intermediates.

4. Making the high-school tennis team, where coaching can be valuable.

5. Entering tennis tourneys on a local level. There are many tournaments on public courts involving hundreds of youths. The age groups of
boys or girls is usually ten and under, twelve and under, fourteen and
under, sixteen and under, eighteen and under. Boys play against boys and
girls against girls.

6. Playing strong grownups.

7.   Registering for high-school meets and club tournaments.

8.   Joining the U.S. Lawn Tennis Association (address: 51 East 42nd St., New York City 10017). A USLTA membership card is necessary for all sanctioned competitions.

9.   Being sufficiently involved in tennis to become a linesman.

10.   Playing in sectional, state, and national championships.

11.   Applying for a tennis scholarship, available to winning competition players at certain colleges.

12.   Making the college team and playing in collegiate matches. The schedule includes team encounters all over North America.

13.   Trying for a berth on the Junior Davis Cup team.

14.   Constantly reading books and studying technical articles about tennis.

15.   Becoming a singles ranking player who will compete in a fixed number of national championships. Good instruction should make this possible.

Coaches insist that a youth's seven to ten years of steady, solid training could take him or her to Forest Hills, and for a few lucky athletes, to the Center court at Wimbledon.

Some adults are not fortunate enough to start at an early age; their best years go into studies and then a career. Competitive tennis begins for certain individuals after their twenty-third or twenty-fifth birthdays. The chances may have been dimmed for top-class competition by then, but at this point it is still possible to become a "B" or even an "A" player. And why not? One can derive deep satisfactions from making the finals in an interclub, intercity, or state tournament, and perhaps even go on to national amateur championships. The climb will be smoothed by private lessons and daily practice, and with vacations spent at tennis resorts or clinics. Tournament opportunities exist all over North America. There are competitive events for men over thirty-five, over forty-five, and over fifty-five or sixty. There are father-son as well as mother-daughter doubles championships, and championships for senior-women singles. In fact, every year some twelve thousand tournaments are held in the United States alone. The tennis magazines and local newspapers announce the dates far enough in advance. Better sporting-goods stores or tennis shops carry the entrance forms.

# TRAITS

Whether adult or adolescent, male or female, all good competitors share certain personality traits. The mental and physical makeup usually runs true to form, and the characteristics show up among the successful of other lands as well.

What makes an outstanding tournament player? Let's sum up some of the necessary assets and qualities:

1. Desire and determination
2. Attitude
3. Thoroughness
4. Ability to concentrate
5. Adaptability
6. Utmost fitness

We may add talent, curiosity, eagerness to acquire still more knowledge, the stubbornness to practice despite setbacks, self-discipline, and the drive for perfection. We also must add aggressiveness; a defensive tennis player can never match a skilled offensive one.

The subject of desirable traits deserves amplification and some actual examples.

Desire is important when you realize that, at first, a competitor reaps few rewards except trophies or newspaper mentions. Yet the pace is often punishing. The average tennis match lasts from one to two hours; three hours are not uncommon. You need plenty of motivation to keep playing for long stretches under humid conditions. (Some competitors lose as much as six to seven pounds in a single day.)

You may have to play while it rains, or the heat waves ooze from the concrete. One coach recalls the training of his two charges: "It was hot that week in Cincinnati, the temperature breaking 100 degrees Fahrenheit in the shade. But each morning I hauled T. and H. onto the courts, making them play six to seven hours of steady hard tennis against each other and various players in the vicinity."

A competitor must possess great measures of will power and a never-diminishing goal, described by one professional athlete as "driving and pushing" yourself relentlessly. "You've got to *want* to win so badly that the thought of coming second is simply intolerable."

A tennis-player's attitude has to be positive, otherwise he won't be able to make the needed personal sacrifices: the daily hours of practice, the turning down of invitations and dates. Ambition and optimism are characteristic for the achievers; they can—and will!—bounce back from a lost match. They want to be the best, sometimes even at the risk of sounding cocky. After becoming a world champion, Stan Smith was asked by reporters about his early goals. Stan Smith replied with candor:

(1) I wanted to be on a Davis Cup team that beat Australia.
(2) I wanted to be Number One player in the U.S.
(3) I wanted to win Wimbledon.
(4) I wanted to become the best player in the world.

Top competitors are much in the limelight—here Stan Smith. *Photo by Art Seitz.*

The will to win goes hand in hand with the right attitude. One's self-confidence cannot waver for an instant, come what may. Genuine competitors won't be influenced by unjust umpires or inattentive linesmen; by unfriendly spectators or the most ferocious adversary.

Roscoe Tanner, the talented super-relaxed American, once explained that the competitor needs "a switch that can turn off everything except the game." Even under great pressure Tanner remains sure of himself, as well as easygoing. The best international professionals know neither fear nor crippling tension. They seldom get rattled, seldom get truly angry (with a few exceptions), seldom show annoyance. They can control their minds. They can shut off worry and isolate themselves even when surrounded by large crowds.

One could find ample proof of self-control among players like Ken Rosewall, Chris Evert, and Billie Jean King, who have been described, in turn, as "deadpan," "a computer," "poker-faced." Arthur Ashe became known as "Mr. Cool" early in his career; Ashe could not be upset by the most hostile crowds or by the trickiest opponents. Thanks to his legendary calmness, he was able to turn near-defeat into victories.

Conversely, some gifted people become so angry that they are no longer able to stroke correctly. One imperious woman was known to snarl at ball boys, and many a game has been lost by impetuous, overly temperamental males. The best tournament players are ice and fire, clear-headed, yet imbued with a fighting spirit, an air of aggressiveness, and an I-want-it-all attitude. One well-known woman pro wears an Indian headband. She fights her adversaries like a warrior who won't give in. She may win four games to nothing, and the set will surely be hers; yet she gives no quarter and makes relentless tennis war even in the last two games. (It is also revealing that good players rarely speak to one another during a match.)

Promising young persons as well as older champions share a thoroughness when it comes to mechanics and technique. If their service needs work, they're conscientious enough to serve a daily three hundred balls (in a row, and alone) for several weeks. They'll spend long hours polishing their strokes, trying to correct the most subtle flaws, consulting and questioning their more experienced friends, and always watching and analyzing competitions. They'll take time off to be alone to replay a lost game in their minds, because they hate to repeat the same tactical error twice.

Future racket stars work at attaining maximum concentration. They cannot allow themselves to be distracted during a game. Rosewall once described one of his younger colleagues as being almost "in a steel box, into which extraneous thoughts could not penetrate." During one of Rosewall's own world-championship games, a woman spectator—one among thousands—had brought a baby, which broke out in periodic fits of crying. Rosewall played his game as though he were deaf.

A brief lapse in concentration may cost several points or an entire game. One veteran amateur learned this the hard way at a western state championship. A psychoanalyst by profession, he had advanced to the state finals, when he was called to the phone. A woman patient was on the line. "I'm going to commit suicide," she told the analyst. "This afternoon! In half an hour!"

The doctor talked her out of it, but on his way back to the court, he began to wonder if he'd really succeeded. Would she kill herself? Since she'd threatened it before—and not done it—the competitor decided to play the important match. The woman had upset him, though. He found it difficult to concentrate and he lost the finals. (His patient had called off the suicide.)

Concentration includes the ability to watch the ball at all times. One racket celebrity was so certain of himself in that department that he offered prizes to photographers who would snap pictures showing him looking elsewhere. The contest ran for years, and apparently each picture proved that the famous eyes *were* on the ball.

Along with fierce concentration and quick thinking, first-rate competitors possess an instinct for the game, along with the brain of a chess master. The best players manage to conceal their shots, making each serve or return a surprise. They're cunning, clever, ready to outwit their opponents, or biding their time to win a point. First-rank competitors are not downcast after an occasional bad day; they accept the dictum that "When you're hot, you're hot; when you're not, you're not." They adapt their thinking processes and strategies to cope with different opponents and different styles. The pros also will adapt themselves to a variety of weather and lighting conditions, and of court surfaces. They may have to play alternately indoors and outdoors; under artificial lights or under a gray windy sky; on concrete, Laykold, clay, or new-fangled plastics.

Moreover, these individuals accept their own capricious metabolisms.

The physical side of the tennis circuit demands stamina and more stamina, fitness and more fitness, and superb health. Tall persons have an edge over short ones, who must run more to reach a ball. Muscled types are less common than wiry ones. Some tennis stars look thin and spindly, and some have narrow shoulders. Yet these athletes of various ages can muster extra reserves when it counts. They'll play five sets a day (or more) at Wimbledon; they may face someone who can be beaten only after hours of almost uninterrupted competition. Billie Jean King and some of her women pros were known to play ten rugged sets every day in various cities and countries, without pause between mid-January and mid-April, with massive amounts of travel in between, and all without signs of exhaustion.

Billie Jean King. *Photo courtesy "Virginia Slims" Circuit.*

These women played themselves into superb physical shape, of course.

By contrast, younger competitors and their peers on the way up would do well not to rely on tennis alone but to pursue (if necessary) an additional daily exercise program.

Who is in shape? One coach defines a physicially fit individual as one "who can play aggressive-offensive defensive tennis continuously for at least 90 to 120 minutes on a daily basis." Experts suggest some of the following exercises to be done every day.

*Running for several miles to increase lung and heart power
*Situps to keep stomach muscles strong for low volley shots
*Pushups to strengthen back and arm muscles used in nearly every stroke
*Wind sprints from base line to net and back (ten times) to improve running speeds
*Knee jumps with knees almost hitting the chest to sharpen reactions. (At least thirty times)

The difference between the physical conditioning of weekend players and competitors lies in the intensity and frequency of the workouts. Some scholastic coaches prescribe preseason programs that include daily twelve minutes of rope jumping (without pause), twelve minutes of running (no rest), plus a series of "hack squats," "calf raises," "jump squats," "bench presses," and dumb-bell exercises. During the competition months, the above regime is slightly reduced. But the trainers encourage their teen-age students to hit the ball for at least four hours a day. (The best junior coaches treat their charges as *individuals* and make sure that the juniors don't get bored or "burned out.")

A competitor's training would be worthless without sensible living habits. Tennis coaches frown upon young people's use of hard liquor (and the overuse by adults). The consumption of nicotine or marijuana are taboo. Tournament players need a balanced food intake. Before a match, they eat lightly. They try to get enough sleep to maintain the speed, force, and good nerves that are essential for tournaments.

# GETTING AHEAD AS A COMPETITOR

Why do some people beat others in their league? Physical attributes such as running ability, quick reflexes, and coordination are only part of the story. Perfect stroke production and intelligent ball placements will account for some won sets. Equally important is the competitor's psychological superiority. He should know his own strengths and must be totally convinced that he (or she) can win, which shows up outwardly as self-assurance. Where does this quality come from?

1. Being in condition
2. Having put in the essential practice hours
3. Bringing the best equipment, including the most suitable racket.

A player should never arrive for a meet with a broken or worn string (carry an extra racket, just in case), or a miniscule crack in a frame. One cannot be self-confident if a button is missing on a tennis garment, or a shoelace has thinned to the breaking point. A competitor must feel like a winner and *look* like one.

If you have already played several matches that day, you need no further warmup; otherwise most coaches suggest some pretournament rallying to take out the kinks, to loosen up, to regroove strokes, and to "oil" the system. The warm-up period can include a friend or coach; the time should not exceed twenty minutes shortly before the actual game. (Tournament players would be wise to avoid waiting in the hot sun or the sauna.)

It is advisable not to arrive *too* early, or one is forced to watch the top-caliber players and the possible winners. One California champion-maker tells his students: "Hanging around the tournament viewing others can make you more nervous. You can lick this. Just appear ten to fifteen minutes before your match."

If you face an equally good player, there may be some psychological ploys to get the better of him (or her), such as the following:

*Using the warm-up period to analyze and probe for weaknesses, while hiding your own weaker shots.

*Starting off with great aggressiveness. Take the immediate offensive and shoot for the other's "Achilles heel." Try to get points right away, but without risks.

*Rushing the net and playing near it whenever you're certain that you can put away a shot. A net appearance gets you "on top" of some people.

*Serving with power into the opponent's weak area. Using effective and forceful smashes.

*Determining the other individual's pace and rhythm and then playing the opposite. If he likes a slow game, "psych" him by playing a fast one, or vice versa.

*"Psyching" the other player by chasing him from base line to net to base line, and across the court as often as possible. Some frustrated competitors lose their cool and thereby the match.

*Making the other person impatient by *returning* every ball. This tactic is a favorite among seniors who no longer want to run hard or play aggressively.

The tennis fraternity doesn't agree on such old "psyching" techniques as waiting too long before serving, taking extra breaks, or telling the other

Rod Laver and Ilie Nastase. *Photos by Art Seitz.*

person, "Here comes another ace" or "Please give me a double fault. I like those . . ." Players use more subtle approaches, such as reassuring their opponents that a ball was "on the line," "almost went out," "missed by three inches," and so on. These remarks can break an adversary's rhythm.

If someone loses too many points, games, and sets, the other person's effectiveness must be lessened. An analytical coach can suggest answers to some common problems:

| PROBLEM | REMEDY |
| --- | --- |
| The other person lobs too much. | Use the smash to discourage him. If you can't smash, make at least some awkward returns so that the other person must run. |
| He is at the net too often. | Lob over his head or keep him busy with cross-court shots. (Lobs are especially effective under artificial lights.) |
| He returns too many serves. | Serve him into the backhand. Vary the serves. Aim for his body or a corner. |
| He wins many points by driving balls at high speeds. | Concentrate on ball before it leaves opponent's racket. Keep ball within eyesight *before* it bounces on your side; anticipate and get your arm back faster. Block the ball. |
| He seems to control the rally. | Take the control away from him when you serve (or come to net and shorten the rally). More important: *Relax!* |
| He seems to get every ball. | Try deep cross courts, short-angle shots, down-the-line shots. Keep him off balance. |
| He never lets you make a strong shot, and concentrates on your weaknesses during the entire game. | You're only as strong as your weakest stroke. Finish the losing game as best you can, then direct your practice at your weak points until they're erased. |

Some basic reminders given at tennis colleges prove useful to advanced buffs, who sometimes forget the *basics.* Here is what one California tennis coach tells them:

*Never start a match without attempting every possible shot in the warm-up period. That means you practice serves, volleys, short angles, deep balls, overheads, half volleys, backhand and forehand groundstrokes, and lobs. Never hit a shot that has no purpose in practice or the match. Disguise your weaknesses, if you can.

*To stroke properly, you need time. You gain it by reacting quickly with your feet and backswing. If your racket is back and your feet are moving to the ball before your opponent's shot reaches the net, you'll gain an extra second.

*Make each stroke perfect; the next shot will take care of itself. Most players cut their strokes short, as though their opponent is simultaneously hitting a shot for which they must prepare themselves. Your follow-through is your only guidance-control system.

# CHAPTER 14

Don Kerbis employs all these instructors. *Photo courtesy Kerbis Tennis Ranches.*

# Tennis Careers

The tennis boom not only brought big profits to tennis-equipment manufacturers and wholesalers, to builders and commercial indoor clubs. The surge in interest also created many new careers; more and more Americans manage to parlay their tennis skills into a solid source of cash. The future looks excellent for court contractors and manufacturers and other well-financed business people. Even a moderately capitalized retail venture stands a chance to succeed. The balance of the 1970s and the '80s should open up many part-time tennis jobs, and provide a full-time livelihood to thousands of persons.

Some of the opportunities are described in this chapter.

# TENNIS SHOP OWNER

The financial success of specialty shops makes sense: Americans in great numbers patronize metropolitan indoor courts, irrespective of season or climate, and the game is perennially popular outdoors in the warmer states on a year-round basis. The customers flock to stores that carry a great variety of tennis equipment and give patient, personal service. The specialty shop is likely to stock items you may need for additional sports, such as backpacking or hiking, fishing, and skiing, to name some examples. How much capital does it take to own a retail outlet? According to industry averages, you cannot open a specialty shop unless you can raise from $40,000 to $100,000. The investment should be backed by an intimate knowledge of the sport, and by at least *some* playing experience. The tennis crowd is sophisticated enough to take its business to the experts; a customer won't come back to someone who can't answer questions about equipment. Retail operations fail because the owner-operator comes from the baseball or football business, and isn't familiar with tennis clothes and fashions. Surveys show that you are best suited for this business if (1) you like meeting the public; (2) your college studies included marketing, economics, accounting or retailing; (3) you have already worked in a store; and (4) you understand the local markets and its special needs. Store ownership can be profitable, particularly in a large city, if you are prepared to work long hours. Specialty tennis shops can also provide modest wages for sales clerks, and young people can sometimes find part-time work as racket stringers.

# TENNIS GOODS BUYER

Department stores, large discount stores, and major sporting-goods dealers employ a person who buys tennis equipment and apparel along with other merchandise. Such positions involve contact with the salesmen; the buyer is also expected to hire and supervise the retail personnel. Salaries range from $8,000 to $20,000 a year, depending on volume and store location. Most tennis-gear buyers generally handle other sporting goods. What with being in charge of several departments, you may have to spend more than an eight-hour day on the job. The work can be pressure-ridden and exhausting.

# TENNIS-RELATED SALESMAN

Racket and ball-machine manufacturers, soft-goods firms, and tennis-court builders all must have representatives who call on wholesalers, retailers, department stores, schools and clubs, or (in the case of private tennis courts) individuals. The earnings of salesmen are related to their products; some men are paid on a commission basis; others get a salary with or without additional commissions. Certain large corporations are not particularly generous to their reps, while some firms ensure an excellent living. (Just compute the sales commission on a tennis court that costs $15,000!)

Opportunities now proliferate for all sorts of tennis-related products, including ball machines. *Photo by Hagood.*

# TENNIS-CLUB MANAGERS

The larger indoor and outdoor tennis clubs need executives to guide and supervise the service to members or customers, count and disburse moneys, hire and pay personnel, buy merchandise, check on the pro shop, and "run" the club on a daily basis. The club executive's remuneration is predicated on the club's size and importance. Some managers receive stock options or a share in the profits; others are paid salaries that approximate those of restaurant-chain managers. To get into tennis-club management, you should have a college degree, a knowledge of the sport, and a pleasant, meet-and-greet-the-public disposition. Club managers generally enjoy more security than prestige. Smaller clubs are less likely to offer positions; such clubs often expect the tennis pro to handle the executive chores.

# RESIDENT PRO

Tennis clubs, country clubs, and large resort hotels employ a "resident pro," who in turn finds suitable instructors, organizes tournaments, supervises a shop, and sees to it that the tennis courts are being maintained. The pro's staff may include a "tennis hostess," who schedules the guests' playing time and finds partners for people who come alone. The resident pro remains on the club or resort scene whether business flourishes or declines during the seasons. Some pros get free housing and long vacations (during the Arizona summer, for instance) plus all or a portion of the pro-shop's profits. The total income depends on your name and fame. (A Pancho Segura usually is well taken care of.) Certain prestigious clubs—the Palm Springs, California, Tennis Club is one illustration—pay higher salaries than small hotels.

Most resident pros consulted for this survey earn from $15,000 to $40,000, with $20,000 being average. (Pros at combination indoor-outdoor clubs make more money than those teaching exclusively outdoors.) The pro position becomes valuable to an aging tennis star. He (or she) need no longer teach to a point of exhaustion; much of the club life can be devoted to socializing. Some older tennis professionals give occasional private lessons or take care of special students, managing to remain for several decades in one club. He (or she) may derive considerable satisfaction from continuity; the pro may have taught a small child who grew into a teen-age competitor and into an adult tennis winner. ("I get much pleasure from teaching the same people year after year," says one pro. "I see them get better and better, and I was the one to help them. I wouldn't be so happy if I got a different crowd every week, as they do in hotels.") Unfortunately, not all resident pros achieve tenure, and some of them lose their jobs for reasons of club politics.

# TENNIS INSTRUCTOR

A tennis instructor, also known as a "teaching pro" may eventually get the coveted job of resident pro. A tennis instructor must possess high technical and personal standards to be considered by a leading club or hired by a first-rate hotel.

Leading American tennis schools like those run by Roy Emerson and Rod Laver or by John Gardiner and Vic Braden select the most technically competent instructors with a proven talent for teaching. Before making an offer, tennis clinics personally test each applicant.

Instructors at tennis ranches and tennis hotels have certain things in common: they look clean-cut; they have agreeable manners (and can communicate); they understand their students' needs and will be tactful with less-gifted or older customers. A long career as a tennis pro may result in arm or foot trouble, which may make it necessary to switch occupations.

Thanks to the tennis explosion, there are not enough qualified, experienced instructors, and promising young players receive many job offers. The pay is fair; it averages about $1,500 per month for experienced teachers whose employment is seasonal, or about $10,000 to $20,000 per year. (Beginners start at $400 to $600.) The sexes have equality, with females standing as good a chance for a job as males. Youth is an advantage to both.

Apart from the salaried teaching pros, "free lancers" sometimes advertise in newspapers and give lessons to young ladies on the courts of apartment complexes or city parks. Their rates vary, as do their abilities, or according to what the market will bear. Finally, some seasonal jobs exist at summer camps for "tennis counselors." Counseling is a nice way to get started in the teaching field.

## TENNIS COACHES

America's universities show a keen interest in tennis, and according to the National Collegiate Athletic Association, most colleges sponsor tennis teams. The demand for full-time tennis coaches should increase on the collegiate level; in addition, high schools are chronically short of *experienced* tennis instructors who can also handle physical education, wrestling, and other sports. (Most high schools cannot afford a full-time tennis coach.) Some teachers receive a special bonus for the extra time to train the tennis team. High-school coaches always earn less than their university colleagues.

## PROFESSIONAL PLAYER

Just as there are many writers but few best-selling ones, so there are many tennis competitors but few who make a financial killing. Indeed, some top-class players refuse to give up their amateur status for many years. They turn down offers to become contract pros and to endorse products for hefty fees. To illustrate: Roy Emerson won every famous event before he finally consented to a pro tour. Arthur Ashe held out until he was twenty-five, and Rod Laver became a touring pro only after he had a family and needed financial security. Thousands of promising amateurs resist the money madness. They play for fun and trophies and make their living through other occupations.

Tennis professionalism doesn't guarantee wealth. Indeed, hundreds hear the call but only few are chosen to earn more on a pro tour than they would as resident club pros. It is true that each year tennis circuits seem to multiply for both men and women, and seasoned competitors can make at least $25,000 to $50,000 a year. It is also true that the prize moneys and various fees of some super stars like Billie Jean King and Stan Smith can add up to $250,000 and more per annum. A big name may receive $1,000 for a tennis demonstration at a store, or direct a two-week tennis clinic for many times that sum. Likewise, the super stars pile up vast incomes from endorsements of

Evonne Goolagong and Margaret Court.
*Photos by Art Seitz.*

products. They give their names to cigarettes (without smoking), to soft drinks or beer (they don't want to drink), or to a tennis racket they may never use. Edwin Fadiman's hard-hitting novel, *The Professional,* paints a realistic picture of the hero's $50,000 contract with a sporting goods firm:

> He was presented with a check and three custom-made steel rackets. The check he turned over to the agent and the bats he put into his room. He still played with his wood racket. He knew he should practice with the steel frames. Truthfully, he didn't like them much. They would play him, he thought, he would not play with them.

A well-known pro endorses one tennis racket in North America, another in Australia, and a third in Europe, and actually gets paid three times. He also will receive money from companies making sunglasses, socks, and toothpaste.

Once they become rich, the stars can get richer by investing wisely in land, real estate, apartment houses, and hotels. The Stan Smiths and Marty Riessens are represented by hard-boiled lawyer-agents who squeeze the business community for various sponsorships. As stars they travel and meet exciting people. They live well.

The aspiring pro should understand, however, that high incomes are restricted to the top rungs of professional tennis. The field is extremely competitive, and to make a living in it, a player needs perfect health, good nerves, and a never-diminishing reservoir of hope. A young world-championship pro can be defeated in his first match and merely win a consolation prize of a few hundred dollars. (He may have to use the check to cover hotel and travel expenses.) The $100,000 purse advertised by a women's pro tour may sound attractive enough; the $100,000 total will be split mostly between the twenty leading (and usually more experienced) competitors, each of whom must play in perhaps a dozen tournaments that week. Sixty other women may end the tour with a slim $500 to $2,000 slice of the big winnings. Newcomers soon realize that professionals must expect a strenuous flight schedule, long training hours, and great stresses while competing. The audience can be large and hostile, and an athlete may get no further than the first round, or to the quarter finals. The six-figure income will be just tennis pie-in-the-sky. In the meantime, even the most modest earnings do not come easily. One observer of the circuits explains the grind:

> The players cannot spend as much time with their families and friends as they would like to. They rush about from airport to airport, from tournament to tournament, packing and unpacking in one hotel room after another, and washing their things at the end of the day. They worry about tickets and passports and currency and excess luggage. They sometimes feel happy and sometimes feel sad—and have to play anyway.

There may be other methods to translate the game into a livelihood. For a few people, it can be the invention of new tennis gadgets or products, or designing tennis clothes. For others, it could be a job in city recreation with a focus on tennis. America's city and state employees may not get rich, but their hours are short and the fringe benefits are considerable.

# PART SIX
## The Passionate Tennis Player

Resort hotels like this one stage many conventions, where guests can play tennis. *Photo by Bob McIntyre.*

# CHAPTER   15

# Where to Improve
# Your Game

As we learned in Chapter 2, there are a number of ways for a player to become more proficient, such as the following:

    *Classes run inexpensively by city recreation departments
    *Classes or tennis clinics held at YMCAs, YWCAs, colleges, and apartment house complexes
    *Tennis clinics run in various cities by "TennisAmerica," a national organization
    *Private or group lessons at indoor or outdoor clubs
    *Summer camps (for children)

You can also polish your technique—or sharpen your strategy—by taking a "tennis vacation." Many better resort hotels, "tennis ranches," second-home or condominium communities, and various vacation centers run clinics that last from two to six days. A typical "Tennis Week" offers the vacationer a package consisting of excellent instruction for all levels, good lodging, and well-cooked meals, plus various other sports. (In some cases, entertainment is added as a bonus.) The majority of the "Tennis Weeks" or short workshops take place in warm states.

The tennis vacation idea was pioneered in the West and Southwest, where you'll find the greatest number of programs.

Region by region, below are some specific tennis travel destinations.

# WEST

## California (North to South)

*Vic Braden's Tennis College,* at Chinquapin, near Tahoe City (Zip 95730), combines superlative week-long group lessons with serene, sunny setting on Lake Tahoe. Accommodations in handsome condominiums with kitchens. Several decades of experience give Braden an edge over his colleagues, who consider him the "dean" of tennis teachers. The Tennis College is for rank beginners, intermediates, and tournament players who want to acquire a complete grasp of tennis and improve their playing ability. Two-day "crash" courses and longer sessions begin in classrooms with stroke demonstrations. Stimulating discussions are led by Braden and two assistant pros. From the classroom, students proceed to the "Braden Teaching Alleys," where automatic ball-pitching machines deliver balls. A camera picks up all the action, which an instructor reviews later on TV screen. Students subsequently test their new knowledge and playing styles on courts. The staff is young, devoted, well-trained, eager. Overall atmosphere first-rate. The college operates from early summer to early fall, with group lessons plus lodging costing you no more than a Caribbean or Hawaiian beach vacation.

The Braden outpost is located twenty-five minutes from Truckee Airport and fifty minutes from Reno International and close to Tahoe airports (accessible via Western Airlines). If driving from San Francisco or Sacramento, take Highway 80 to Highway 89, then Highway 28 to Chinquapin. Rental cars plus inexpensive bus shuttles available at Reno International Airport.

Across the lake, you'll find the *TennisAmerica Tennis Center* at Incline

Village (89450). The fourteen-court, six-acre complex is busy with clinics during the summer. The use of modern equipment includes video tapes. An eighteen-hole golf course, hiking, fishing, water skiing, boating, and gaming make for a complete vacation.

*John Gardiner's Tennis Ranch,* Box 155, Carmel Valley (93924), is south of San Francisco in a nest of trees, flowers, and hillsides. Here is where the tennis vacation idea began (in 1957), and has never been quite duplicated by anyone else in the same sybaritic, hedonistic style: assorted fresh fruit and berries for breakfast, fresh-squeezed juices frequently brought courtside by immaculate waiters. Elegant lunches for the diet-conscious and dinners for gourmet. The ranch is small, intimate, refined, for couples only, with emphasis on superior tennis instruction (ratio: four pupils to one teacher). Massages, whirlpools, swims. This Gardiner enclave has been called "The Tiffany of Tennis" and a five-day week is priced accordingly.

*La Costa Resort Hotel and Spa,* at Rancho La Costa (92008), spread out near the costal highway about two hours south of Los Angeles and thirty minutes north of San Diego. Private instruction on more than two dozen all-weather courts, with lessons supervised by Pancho Segura. Every type of deluxe accommodation from rented villa to private rooms, plus vast resort with high rates. World-class players and Hollywood notables come to tournaments at the La Costa, where famous golf events take place too. The complex includes huge swimming pools, stables, ladies' beauty treatments, massages, gyms, Cordon Bleu dining, and all-in "spa" (beauty farm) rates that soon will reach $100 per per night. The La Costa is often fully booked with conventions. Reserve far in advance. Year-round.

*Rancho Bernardo,* 17550 Bernardo Oaks Drive, San Diego (92128), overlooks green, climate-blessed hillsides, some thirty minutes from San Diego (limousine service available). Rancho Bernardo is a recreational community with handsome, affordable resort beds. The inn sells a tennis package including day-long lessons at fair rates, with ball machines and audio-visual aids, plus a good room. The course can be taken on two week days, on a weekend, or for longer periods, depending on the student.

The Rancho "Learning Center" caters to every type of player. The Rancho Bernardo Inn also offers an eighteen-hole golf course, two heated swimming pools, horseback riding, table tennis, shuffleboard, bike rentals, well-appointed old world restaurants, and a modern shopping plaza. The Rancho is often booked to capacity with conventions.

Other San Diego places where one can obtain lodging and enjoy club tennis facilities are the *El Camino Tennis Club,* in Oceanside, The *Kona Kai Club,* on San Diego's Shelter Island, *Vacation Village,* in Mission Bay, and the historic stately *Hotel Del Coronado* at Coronado (92118). Although the Coronado is primarily a convention hotel, it will appeal to tennis players, who can take lessons on a dozen outdoor courts that overlook the Pacific Ocean. Periodically offered packages include private instruction and rooms at nonexorbitant rates. At the hotel's marina, you see a fleet of deep-sea fishing vessels and sailing ships. The nonfishing guest can enjoy the eighteen-hole golf course, a health spa, along with San Diego sightseeing.

*The Tennis Club,* 701 West Baristo Road in Palm Springs (92262), attracts tennis connoisseurs in search of tasteful bungalows (each with its own patio), private lessons from a distinguished resident pro and his seasoned staff. The dozen outdoor courts are surrounded by palms, bougainvillea and other tropical vegetation at the base of many-hued hillsides. Fine swimming pool and free whirlpools. A tennis hostess matches up players who arrive alone. Further company can be found in the club's sociable cocktail lounges and on outdoor terraces. Above-average dining, quiet winter-spring vacation atmosphere at edge of Palm Springs. The Tennis Club should not be confused with Palm Springs' ultra-exclusive Racquet Club. The latter resembles a pedigree-conscious country club that goes in more for fashion shows, charity balls, jewelry-displaying ladies.

*Vic Braden's Tennis College,* 45–730 San Louis Rey, Palm Desert (92260), is part of the eighty-acre Shadow Mountain Resort and Racquet Club. Braden offers two-, three-, and five-day courses at the College on a dozen courts, with sixteen "Braden Teaching Lanes," a Video-Tape Analysis center, a classroom. The Racquet Club has night tennis, a sauna, swimming pools, and excellent accommodations (some with cooking facilities). It should be remembered that Braden introduced the idea of "tennis colleges," and that the course is a worthwhile investment. Palm Desert is only a short drive from the Palm Springs airport, where the customers can land with Western Airline jets. (Western also connects the tennis vacationer with the bright lights of Las Vegas, Nevada. Here tennis instruction is available at most major hotels on the "Strip.")

*Vic Braden's Tennis College, Coto de Caza,* Trabuco Canyon, (92678) is set amid 5,000 acres of the Santa Ana Mountains, meadows, and rolling hills. The backyard includes such well-known California recreation areas of Laguna, Balboa, and Newport. Horseback riding, hunting, and a sports complex with handball, basketball, bowling, and elaborate equestrian facility with 30 miles of open trails, a hunt lodge and fields of game birds, trap and skeet shooting, an Olympic pool, three separate dining areas, and children's recreation area. Coto is the permanent headquarters of the Braden Colleges. Championship lighted courts with multiple court video capacity from a central tower, sixteen fully-automated Braden Teaching Lanes, a Video-Analysis Center, a classroom featuring multiple front and rear-view audio-visual aids, and on-court instructional machines and targets. Coto de Caza is 30 minutes from Orange County Airport and ninety from Los Angeles International. Housing in luxury condominium rooms. Costs of the Tennis College comparable to the other Braden Tennis College locations. Coto also offers *Tennis Academy* for tennis professionals who learn how to teach.

## Idaho

*Sun Valley Tennis School, Sun Valley* (83353), first became known for its children's programs and young-adult summer tennis camps. It is also for adults of all playing levels, including beginners. Each course consists of instruction for five consecutive days. Each day is divided into two ninety-minute sessions. Since the lessons are private, a student can start any time during the season and stretch the "course" over seven days. Rates for the five days are high, as one might expect in one of the West's most prestigious and remote resorts. Sleeping possibilities range from $100-per-night condominiums to single rooms in the Sun Valley complex. Restaurants and other sports abound. Sun Valley is tucked away in the foothills of the Sawtooth Mountains of central Idaho, 85 miles from Twin Falls, Idaho, 155 miles from Boise, Idaho, and 300 miles from Salt Lake City.

## Colorado

*Cliff Buchholz Tennis School,* at "The Timbers," Steamboat Springs (80477), offers week-long vacation clinics (summers only). Good-humored, well-run instruction will advance a beginner toward match play in record time, thanks to assorted drills and games. Experienced tennis buffs profit from the strategy sessions, and the special high-altitude training. The school comprises a $350,000 indoor facility with permanently mounted video cameras, a modern classroom for lectures and films, an indoor court for teaching and video analysis. Ample outdoor facilities, pro shop, pool. Other diversions include horseback riding, jeeping, fishing, hiking. Students stay at the wood-and-stone "Timbers Lodge," which overlooks the valley. (Bring sun cream and insect repellent.) All-round ambience excellent for singles. Fair package prices include lodging, dining (extensive menu), and a cocktail party. Buchholz also runs camps for juniors at same location at different dates.

*Snowmass Resort,* ten miles from Aspen (81654), consists of large, luxurious lodges, condominiums, apartments. (Average resort prices for quality lodging.) You play tennis on Laykold surfaced courts. Complete club house facilities available adjacent to courts. Tennis pro available for lessons and to set up tournaments. Write Snowmass Reservations, at above address.

*Broadmoor Hotel,* six miles south of Colorado Springs (80901), remains outstanding for tennis vacationers, despite the many conventions. The Mobil Guide top rating only goes to a few resort hotels. The Broadmoor is one of the few, and the prices are commensurate. You take tennis lessons on the Broadmoor's many outdoor and indoor courts. You can play golf here for 330 days a year on two eighteen-hole courses, which are part of the Broadmoor's five thousand lusciously landscaped acres. You skate in the hotel's World Arena. You swim in an all-year, glass-walled Olympic-size outdoor pool. Guests sip cocktails in four bars, including an eighteenth-century English pub. The Penrose Dining room commands a view of Pikes Peak, and has the most renowned European cuisine in the state.

*The John Gardiner Tennis Club* at Keystone can be found at the Keystone Ski Area two driving hours, 72 miles west of Denver. (Post office: Dillon, Colorado 80435) The Keystone tennis facility utilizes this excellent winter sports' center's condominiums, lodges, and motels.

The Gardiner Club consists of a dozen outdoor and two indoor championship courts, a full pro shop with equipment and clothing, a club house with showers and sauna.

The tennis professionals are groomed by John Gardiner. Teaching is strengthened by the use of video-tape equipment for instant replay and ball machines.

Colorado's tennis destinations include (among others) the *Four Seasons Village* and its tennis courts at Breckenridge, about a two-hour drive (eighty-six miles) from Denver. (Lessons available. Pro shop.) Condominiums for couples or larger groups. You can also play tennis at the *C Lazy U Ranch,* in Granby, and courts can be rented in the attractive, expensive resort community of Vail. (Write J. Staufer, Vail Village Inn, Vail (81601).

# THE MIDWEST

## Michigan

*Don Kerbis Tennis Ranch,* Watervliet (49098), is noted for its extensive and expertly run tennis camps for boys and girls (minimum age 10). Don Kerbis' name is also associated with unusual five-day adult clinics. These are crammed with stroke-production reviews, station drills, games, tournaments (sixteen courts). Somewhat removed from civilization, Kerbis' colony doesn't resemble other tennis outposts; A bugle sounds reveille at 8 A.M.; before

At the Kerbis Ranch.

breakfast phys-ed teachers lead you on jogs and encourage calisthenics. The majority of the housing consists of bunk beds in army-style barracks (with a separation of the sexes), but there are also some A-frame dwellings for customers who refuse to rough it. Adequate simple food and congenial atmosphere. Horseback rides, pool swimming, and long evening conversations add to the camp mystique. International staff headed by the dynamic Don Kerbis. Reasonable package rates. The tennis ranch is surrounded by 120 acres of thick forest and farmland. It takes about two hours to drive the one hundred miles from Chicago, Illinois. Not far away from Kerbis, *Michigan Shores Tennis Academy,* at South Haven, Michigan (49090), organizes tennis vacation weekends on its twenty courts in a 45-acre forest preserve. Meals and room plus other sports included in rates.

## Missouri

*Lodge of the Four Seasons,* at Lake Ozark (65049), features more than two dozen courts in a resort that emphasizes gourmet dining, a nightclub and several bars, shopping, sightseeing. The tennis facilities (lessons available) are complemented by fishing, hunting, riding, golf, swimming, a health spa. The lodge is off State Highway 54, some 170 miles southwest of St. Louis, 170 miles southeast of Kansas City. Flights to Lake of Ozarks airport.

## Indiana

*French Lick Sheraton Hotel and Country Club,* in French Lick (47432), has a high rating among tennis vacationers who return to this 1,600-acre estate every year. Apart from the racket activity, you find golfing on two eighteen-hole courses, bowling, swimming, skating, many other sports. The 500-room hotel's elegance is matched by elegant prices. While in Indianapolis, inquire about the Ramey Tennis School.

# SOUTH AND SOUTHWEST

## Texas

*Laver-Emerson Tennis Weeks,* 9800 Northwest Freeway, Houston (77018), take place in a woodsy clean-air retreat at April Sound, on Lake

Conroe, half an hour from Houston (limousine service for guests). Unlike other tennis clinics headed by famous players, Roy Emerson or Rod Laver are *always* in attendance, personally teaching all day long, challenging the guests to games and directing a staff of superb instructors who grade the students upon arrival. In addition to week-long clinics, there are two-day crash courses that transform the total newcomer into a player. The two Australian stars' personalities suffuse the cheerful teaching. (Ratio: one instructor to as few as three students.) Well-maintained outdoor and covered courts available to tourists all year. Tennis weeks and clinics restricted to spring and fall, when Texas shows its best climatic face. Activities include socializing with Emerson and friends, after-hours contact with instructors, swimming, saunas, boating (man-made lake), discotheque, bar. Accommodations in attractive apartments and good food (including one ten-course dinner) included in package. An exceptional tennis experience.

An Arizona tennis ranch is one ideal place to become a good player. *Photo courtesy Markow Photography for Gardiner Tennis Ranches.*

*T-Bar-M Tennis Ranch,* New Braunfels (78130), is more isolated and more primitive, with motel style, cottage, and bunkhouse accommodations. New Braunfels was founded by German settlers in 1845. The ranch occasionally runs tennis clinics for ladies only, as well as instruction for couples.

*Lakeway Inn,* twenty miles from Austin, Texas, offers complete hotel facilities, which are occupied by a steady stream of conventions. Tennis activity on a record number of courts. The Austin area gets unbearably hot in summer and should be considered unsuitable for vacations.

## Arizona

*John Gardiner Tennis Ranch,* in Scottsdale, (Phoenix) (85253), is the flagship and star of Gardiner's far-reaching empire. The mauve Camelback Mountain, the lush plants and flowers enhance a lovely scene compounded of tennis couples or singles in white, a dozen green terraced courts and the tanned staff. The tennis industry regards this ranch as the "West Point of Tennis," and the program is taken ultra-seriously. Five-day clinics and shorter sessions scientifically planned by John Gardiner, who believes in ample modern ball machines, filming with closed-circuit TV, a top-notch staff, free Swedish massages, and an award-winning dining room (famous cuisine). The overall Tennis Ranch atmosphere reminds one of an active, attractive glamorous country club with adjacent villas (or "casitas") scattered, Acapulco-style over the mountain. The package rate may be high but it buys guaranteed tennis improvement and a quality vacation. (October through May only.) The Scottsdale-Phoenix area also appeals to tennis vacationers who require no clinic but just occasional lessons. *Arizona Biltmore Hotel,* in Phoenix (85002), has long been the traditional oasis for recreational players. Five-day rates comprise a lesson a day, plus superlative accommodations and food. Hourly fees on the dozen Plexipave courts. The Arizona Biltmore shines with many resort features. A beautiful setting among flowers and cacti. Winter rates are high. The Scottsdale *Hilton Inn* offers a half-dozen courts, employs a pro, and has earned a reputation for efficient management and a friendly, personal touch. The Scottsdale *Camelback Inn* offers free playing privileges to guests,

In the clear, dry air of sunny Scottsdale, tennis is a popular year-round sport at various hotels. Bright arc lights keep the courts almost daylight-bright after sundown, making it possible to enjoy a good game or lesson from the pro late in the evening. *Photo courtesy Bowerman-Camelback Inn, Scottsdale, Arizona.*

who can avail themselves of lessons. The Marriott-owned motel-style inn also comes alive with beauty clinics, horseback rides, fashion shows, cocktail parties, steak fry rides, nightly dancing. Phoenix is accessible via Western Airlines and other carriers.

*Racquet Club Ranch,* in Tucson (85716) houses tennis vacationers in deluxe modern apartments with fully equipped kitchens, color TV, fireplace, beamed ceilings, carpeting throughout. Guests who do not wish to cook can have supper at the Ranch restaurant. Winter tennis clinics of various lengths are headed by name players. Conditioning program, instruction via TV playback in all strokes, lectures and lessons in singles and doubles strategy. Thirty-four Laykold outdoor courts can be lighted for night playing. Olympic pool and other amenities.

## Alabama and Georgia

*Grand Hotel,* at Point Clear, Alabama (36564), shares its landscaped acreage with Lakewood Tennis Club. Eight Rubico courts (requiring white attire), various tennis programs for adults and children headed by Charlene Grafton and staff. Good pro shop. The hotel's magnificent location on the Gulf of Mexico means sandy beaches, deep-sea fishing, water skiing, boating and sailing. Swimming, horseback riding, skeet and trap shooting. American-plan rates apply to the many different kinds of accommodations, at expected deluxe rates. (Some package plans.) Year-round operation. Planes land at Point Clear or at Mobile, Alabama, fifty miles from the hotel. Limousines.

*Cloister Resort,* on Sea Island, Georgia (31561), stands out among the cognoscenti for its aristocratic ambience and suave service, along with sports of every kind. The trade includes honeymooners and statesmen. More than a dozen well-kept courts. Expensive.

## Florida

*Bay Hill Club and Lodge,* in Orlando (32811), is a lavish Florida-style club that accepts nonmembers at daily modified American-plan rates. (Reservation by mail or a reference useful.) The lodge accommodations are spacious, comfortably furnished with two beds, fully air-conditioned and heated, with color television and direct-dial telephone service. Complete dining facilities. Several excellent all-weather courts; lessons available from Todd Harris, long-time tennis pro for Arnold Palmer. Average prices. Summer rates drop as the Florida temperature goes up. The Orlando resort also excels in golf and other sports.

*Boca Raton Hotel and Club,* in Boca Raton (33432), built up its tennis facilities through the years. More than a dozen courts are kept busy in winter. Well-known pro. The hotel attracts important tennis tournaments. The large *Innisbrook Resort,* in Tarpon Springs (33589), offers several hard- and soft-surface courts. Guests can play at no charge; reservations required and court time limited to ninety minutes. A full-time pro plus tennis shop. The Innisbrook resort also receives praise from golfers.

*Laver-Emerson Tennis Center,* at Delray Beach (33444), is some forty-four miles (or about an hour's motoring) north of Miami. Tennis students have access to two-dozen courts, a pro shop, a club house. They're housed in handsome villas and condominiums. The Center offers the two Australian players' well-planned seasonal "Tennis Weeks," with either Roy Emerson or Rod Laver personally present to dramatize the lessons. Congenial.

*Fountainebleau Hotel,* in Miami Beach (33140), has many courts and a permanent teaching staff. The Fountainebleau goes in for exhibitions and a number of amateur and famous pro events under the eyes of ex-champion Gardnar Mulloy. The Fountainebleau remains among the largest and busiest hotels in Florida, with the annexes adding up to a massive array of rooms and activities.

*Colony Beach and Tennis Club,* near Sarasota (33578), appeals to tennis players because of its numerous outdoor courts, a reliable resident pro, various visiting tennis celebrities, plus accommodations and an ocean-front location. High winter rates. Sightseeing possibilities. Lastly, the estatelike *Belleview Biltmore,* at Clearwater, Florida, should be mentioned for its seventy-five years as a complete resort. This includes tennis on a half-dozen courts. Short season. Closed in summer.

# THE EAST

## West Virginia

*Greenbrier,* at White Sulphur Springs, West Virginia (24986), distinguishes itself from other well-known spas by its incomparable class and style. The hotel's gardens remind one of Versailles. The dining cannot be surpassed. Tennis on an adequate number of porous and hard courts, with an adjacent pro shop and competent instruction. (Other sports available, too.) The Greenbrier tariff is commensurate with its fame. Expensive and formal.

## New England

*Woodstock Inn* is located in Woodstock, Vermont (05091) The Inn also manages the Woodstock Country Club, where guests play on six clay courts and two all-weather courts. Use fees approximate to those charged by many indoor courts for both singles and doubles. Nonguests pay more and must make reservations. The tennis rectangles and the Woodstock Country Club are just a half-mile from the Inn. This Rockefeller-owned resort hotel deserves its reputation for dignity, intimacy, service. Woodstock's location encourages hiking and other sports. Travelers who come to Vermont in groups or with large families might consider the *Snow Lake Lodge,* at Mt. Snow, Vt. (05356) which doubles as a mass-market ski area during the winter. In summer there are eight tennis courts for group or individual lessons. Some week-long clinics on a double occupancy basis. The aging but still elegant *Mt. Washington Hotel,* at Bretton Woods, New Hampshire (03575), hosts occasional vacation clinics on its dozen red-clay courts. Fishing, golf, horseback

Good hotels—east or west—usually have tennis courts. *Photo by Julie Warn.*

riding, trail walks are additional attractions. *Wentworth-by-the-Sea* is also in New Hampshire, close to Portsmouth (03801), and affords nearby ocean swimming. Lively summer season on the hotel's clay courts. Elegant. While on Cape Cod, tennis vacationers often chose the *Blue Water Resort,* which overlooks the blue ocean in Bass River, Massachusetts (02664). (Distance to Boston: seventy-five miles.) The resort is away from traffic. The management provides all the comforts, even special bags and ice in your room to soothe a possible tennis elbow.

## New Jersey and New York

*Tennis America Tennis Weeks,* at Lawrenceville, New Jersey (06648), some five miles south of Princeton, New Jersey, were originally for juniors (ages ten to seventeen). The Lawrenceville complex organizes special tennis sessions for adults as well. (Inquire about dates.) In addition to two-dozen courts, the 360-acre campus has a golf course, fields for football and soccer, a running track, a field house. The tennis program consists of first-rate instruction video taping, expert analysis.

*Mohonk Mountain House,* New Paltz, New York (12561), is a fine old Victorian establishment with a number of clay courts plus pro. The vacationer is treated to quality in the formal, castle-like lodge. American-plan rates in proportion with setting.

*Concord,* at Kiamesha Lake, N. Y. (12751), is one of those enormous 1,300-room resorts in the Catskills, where New Yorkers seek temporary escape from the extreme summer heat. The hotel may be best known for its Jewish food, famous nightclubs (a half-dozen orchestras perform sometimes simultaneously), well-advertised special weekends. The tennis player should not underestimate the facilities. These have increased steadily through the years. By the end of the 1970s, there'll be the grand total of two-dozen indoor courts and nearly a dozen outdoor courts. Tournaments of all sorts. Pro and pro shop. A busy resort. *Grossingers Hotel,* at Grossinger, N. Y. (12734), is only a third as large as the Concord and features less tennis courts, too. But the extras match those of other meccas: indoor and outdoor pools, golf, health club, social director, games and entertainment of every kind, plus kosher food.

# THE CAROLINAS

## South Carolina

Imagine an island, complete with sand beaches en masse, palm trees, mystic Southern forests, almost year-round warmth, with inns, condominiums, villas, elegant homes, parks, a 600-acre forest preserve, and a wildlife sanctuary. The above plus a fanatic devotion to the game of tennis characterize *Hilton Head Island,* South Carolina (29928). The picture can stand some amplification. For one thing, Hilton Head endorses not just tennis on several courts but also a pollution-free, to-be-conserved background. (Ecologists rave about the island.) For another thing, the entire isle seems to dedicate itself to the vacationer and second-home owner, who demand manifold other sports as well. You'll therefore find marinas and sailing schools, deep seafishing, a dozen golf courses, stables filled with horses for riding, bicycle rentals, ultra-clean beaches and of course, swimming pools. The island-associated golfers (Jack Nicklaus and Arnold Palmer) are as famous as the tennis personages who represent Hilton Head, among them Stan Smith, the Wimbledon winner and Billie Jean King. For prospective guests, the lineup is as follows:

*The Hilton Head Racquet Club* became famous for Billie Jean King who lent her name to this resort and supervised some of the designs. The Club provides day and night play on almost two-dozen assorted courts. Hourly playing fees are high, with rates for accommodations to match. (Guests sleep in nearby villas and condominium apartments.) The clubhouse, swimming pool, and other expected facilities are all equally luxurious.

Hilton Head's 4000-acre *Sea Pines Plantation* (same zip) has Stanley R. Smith (or Stan Smith for short) as its figurehead. The tennis school of the Plantation's "Harbor Town" Racquet Club is headed by other individuals and a corps of instructors. More than two-dozen clay-type courts and practice facilities serve noted international championships; the tennis layout is complemented by sizeable golf links. Several hundred villas accommodate the tennis vacationers and their families in great style and at a price. (Weekly rates available.) There is also room at the motel-like *Port Royal Inn,* which charges at the peak season from $40 to $50 per day with two meals. The Sea Pines Plantation has a picture book quality; the tableau contains among other nautical symbols an attractive lighthouse. "Blissfully free of custard stands," comments one tennis writer in summing up the area's appeal.

*The Palmetto Dunes Racquet Club* consists of townhouses and an inn with restaurants, cocktail lounges, shops and an endless sand beach. Golf and boating provide a change from tennis, which is played here on a dozen close courts. (Modern videotape equipment and first-rate instruction.) The club is favored by persons who prefer proximity to courts.

The *Tennis America* Adult Clinic at *Port Royal Plantation,* takes the sport seriously, and drills its students on several courts during much of spring and summer. Instruction for every type of player on a lush island which boasts many interesting restaurants amid tropical flora.

## North Carolina

The *High Hampton Inn and Country Club,* Cashiers, N. C. 28717, about 60 miles south of Asheville, N. C. commands a view of hillsides and trees, wildflowers and meadows, lakes and golf courses. Tennis on seven courts. Occasional clinics. The *Grove Park Inn* at Asheville (28802) has a lovely mountain setting, too, plus four courts and a resident pro.

# THE CARIBBEAN AND MEXICO

*The* (300-room) *Dorado Beach Hotel* is located twenty miles west of San Juan, Puerto Rico, on the north shore of the island. There are seven all-weather tennis courts, and several teaching pros. Reasonable court fees for hotel guests.

*Cerromar Beach Hotel* is a mile down the beach from the Dorado. This 503-room resort has a dozen all-weather courts (some lighted for night play).

Two assistant pros on hand for lessons. Tennis packages available. Both hotels have fine golf courses.

*Caneel Bay Plantation,* on St. John in the U.S. Virgin Islands, hugs the Virgin Islands National Park. This 130-room resort features several all-weather courts. (No fees for registered guests.) This is an extraordinarily plush Rockefeller-built hostelry with excellent service.

The 777-room *Princess Hotel,* in Acapulco, Mexico and its beachside sister hotel, the *Pierre Marques,* offer guests more than a dozen courts. The Acapulco Princess has eight, two of which are indoors and air-conditioned. All the outdoor facilities are lighted for night play. (High indoor rates in winter.) A special tennis deal includes free use of the outdoor courts, one private lesson, an hour's indoor play, cocktails. The Acapulco Princess was built in the shape of an Aztec pyramid; its architecture and grounds are remarkable. Tennis vacationers will welcome the hotel's isolation from an otherwise touristy and brassy Mexican resort.

More information about hotels with large tennis facilities in Mexico and the Caribbean can be obtained by writing to:

Western International Hotels, The Olympic, Seattle, Wash. 08111
Inter-Continental Hotels, Box 1456, South Miami, Fla. 33143
Sheraton Hotels, Box 1044, Boston, Mass. 02103

# CHAPTER 16

# A Short History of Tennis

Did tennis—or an activity that resembled it—originate in Greece, as some sports historians claim? There seems to exist precious little proof, nor do we have evidence that the origins go back to Rome. Some first illustrations and descriptions come to us from thirteenth-century France, where members of the royal court invented a new diversion: they propelled a small ball to one another, using their palms. They called it *le jeu de paume, jeu* meaning game and a *paume* being the palm. The French clergy took up this recreation as happily as King Louis IX himself. Reliable accounts tell us, however, that in 1245, the French king considered the *jeu* beneath the dignity of priests and monks, and decreed that tennis was henceforth forbidden for the clergy. At about the same time, a Rouen archbishop ordered that such goings on had to stop in the monasteries. Louis X (1289–1316) upheld the law, although he played tennis himself until a few days before his death.

Some time between 1358 and 1360, English visitors to France were sufficiently impressed to bring "court tennis" back to their island. King Edward III (1312–1377), was fighting the French at sea and on land, sacking the cities of Normandy and battling the Scots, and still found time to have a tennis court built in his palace. A famous reveler and innovator, Edward liked the game; so did poet Geoffrey Chaucer and his contemporaries.

References to tennis turn up through English history and literature; even Shakespeare alluded to it in Act I of *Henry V,* written in about 1599:

> When we have match'd our rackets to these balls
> We will in France, by God's grace, play a set.

Henry VIII of England built some splendid courts that still survive in London. The Elizabethans were joined by the ruling classes of other nations. King Philip of Spain engaged in this royal pastime and the Italian nobles amused themselves in the same manner. An Italian priest wrote an impressive book on the subject in 1655; fifty years later, the French may have had some two thousand courts in their land, mostly in and near Paris. The court dimensions varied, and so did the sites, which could be indoors or outdoors, on natural soil, or paved with cobbles. The leather balls, at first stuffed with human hair, eventually contained wool; bare hands and gloved hands were relieved by paddles.

Court tennis could be played against walls, across wooden barricades, or over earth mounds; eventually ropes and then primitive rope nets also made good barriers.

Fashions change, and by the eighteenth century, the royal gentry had lost interest in the game. Weeds grew on the former playgrounds for which other uses were found. But in the 1860s, we encounter once more traces of tennis-like activities, this time on the green lawns of Essex and Roxburgshire. Around 1872, for example, the Leamington Croquet Club utilized a rectangular meadow in Leyton, Essex. Croquet was popular just then; badminton had been imported from India, and the squashlike "racquets" was being played in Harrow and Eton and other schools.

It took an enterprising, energetic Englishman-sportsman to blend elements from all these games, add a touch of the medieval-court tennis, devise a complicated, new sixty-foot-long grassy area (thirty-foot at the base line but less at the net). It was labeled with the almost unpronounceable Greek word for ballplaying, *Sphairistike.* The enterpreneur was Major Walter Clopton Wingfield, military man, horseman, and country gentleman.

On a cool December afternoon in 1873, Wingfield introduced lawn tennis at a garden party. To his friends, acquaintances, and British society, he issued an eight-page pamphlet that explained scoring methods and rules, including a chivalrous one: ladies were allowed to serve nearer the net than men. A patent was granted Wingfield on February 23, 1874, and the promoter had a firm manufacture suitable tennis sets. These consisted of wood, cat-gut-strung paddles with long wooden handles; small, hollow rubber balls; nets; and netposts. Wingfield was proclaimed the "inventor" over the protests of some individuals in other parts of England. In any case, English society was happy with the novelty, and the tennis outfits wandered merrily to other countries. Soon rubber balls flew wherever there were mansions with lawns.

Moreover, one June day of 1877, a notice appeared in a British journal about "a lawn tennis meeting," open to all amateurs, with "a gold prize for the winner and silver to the second player." Balls could be obtained by "personal application to the gardener." Wimbledon drew twenty-two players for this first tournament.

Tennis now caught on modestly in the British Isles. A visitor to Britain brought the equipment back to Bermuda, where he lived. The lawn-tennis idea found an eager supporter in Sir Brownlow Gray, who staked out a grass court on the grounds behind his home in Paget. Sir Brownlow eventually became too busy as a chief justice of Bermuda, but his daughter and her friends began to play, spreading the popularity throughout the Caribbean. Mary Brownlow's name shows up in the first Bermudan tournaments. Scoring was different then. A game constituted fifteen points and on reaching fourteen a player would shout "Game ball!"

Sports historians seem to agree that it took a young lady from Staten Island, New York, to bring lawn tennis to Americans. Mary Ewing Outer-

Paget, Bermuda—1893. Mixed doubles at Cleremont, then the home of the late Sir Brownlow and Lady Grey. This tennis court, laid out in 1873, was the first in the Western Hemisphere.

bridge visited Bermuda to spend a holiday with relatives. During her visit she was invited to play the new game with officers of the British garrison stationed in Bermuda. At that time the garrison included units from the Royal Artillery, the Royal Engineers, the 53rd Regiment (the King's Shropshire Light Infantry) and the 69th Regiment (the South Lincolnshires later became the 2nd Batallion of the Welsh Regiment).

The game obviously fascinated young Mary and she reached a sufficient degree of skill to acquire from regimental stores a net, balls, and rackets, which she carried back to New York with her when she sailed on the S.S. *Canima.*

The date of Miss Outerbridge's return to the United States has been set variously at January 12, 1874, or March 4, 1874. (The March sailing seems more likely.) At all events, Mary Outerbridge prodded a brother to stake out a tennis court on the lawns of the Staten Island Cricket Club, where the family had a membership.

According to Staten Island Historical Society, "Mary Outerbridge's girl friends took up the recreation with reluctance, not being sure it was 'ladylike' to go racing and leaping in pursuit of a flying, bouncing ball." However, on days when the men engaged in cricket, the girls took part in the holiday amusements by playing tennis.

The Outerbridge boys soon recognized that lawn tennis offered plenty of speed and precision. The sons played and influenced their men friends to join them. Before long, the game became popular among the Staten Island set.

During roughly the same period, lawn-tennis courts sprang into action at Nahant, Massachusetts, and on estates in Newport, Rhode Island, and Plainfield, New Jersey. The sudden popularity meant more competitive play, and the first tournament took place in September 1880 on the Outerbridge's Cricket Club grounds. Tennis had established a firm hold among America's high and the mighty, especially the mining and railroad barons.

Courts were set up to accommodate the smart sets of Boston, Philadelphia, and New York. Thanks to Major Wingfield's foresight and Mary Outerbridge's enthusiasm, many ladies flocked to play on the turf. Female and male play styles differed little just then, with the ball soaring over a shoulder-high net. The grass was good for everyone's feet, and listeners were treated to the exclamation "Love! Love!" The game earned some derision for these calls and for the game's initial softness; a Harvard University fellow commented that "men who have rowed should blush to be seen playing Lawn Tennis." But the sport's acceptance kept growing among the elite, which included the class-conscious establishment of Newport, Rhode Island. Society flocked to the Newport Casino, where the ladies in ankle-length skirts and petticoats, in wide hats topped by parasols, watched wealthy men dash across the green surfaces in long, striped pants, with striped caps to match. Some of the gentry sported knickerbockers and business shirts. We see similar scenes in New Brighton, Staten Island, New York, and Germantown, Pennsylvania, and on the elegant grounds of the Philadelphia Cricket Club.

Californians took the cue and built their own courts; tennis was now

What the tennis player wore in 1894, Miss Low's School, Stamford, Conn.
*Photo courtesy Mrs. T. Campbell.*

played in Ontario, Canada, and in Montreal. Several dozen social and sports clubs, once mainly devoted to cricket, added this new diversion, and while tea was being served to the wives, their gents in handlebar moustaches flung balls across the grass courts. Rules varied from area to area, and in 1881, representatives from various clubs banded together to issue a call for the first meeting of the United States National Lawn Tennis Association.

The letter that was the beginning of organized tennis in the United States, read as follows:

It is proposed to hold a lawn tennis convention in New York about the middle of May for the purpose of adopting a code of rules and designating a standard ball, to govern and be used in all lawn table matches or tournaments throughout the United States, with a view of enabling all clubs or individual players to meet under equal advantages.

A permanent organization will be formed under the name of the "United States Lawn Tennis Association," in which name the rules adopted at the convention will be issued. All regularly organized tennis clubs, or other clubs which number tennis among their games, are invited to send representatives to the convention. Clubs may send from one to three representatives, but no club shall have more than three, and each club shall be entitled to one vote only. Representatives must bring credentials, signed by the secretary of the club which they represent. The undersigned clubs have organized this movement at the urgent request of the most prominent players in their respective districts, and the necessity of

Ladies at play in 1894, Miss Low's School, Stamford, Conn. *Photo courtesy Mrs. T. Campbell.*

such action will be appreciated by all who take an interest in inter-club, inter-State, or international matches.

It is hoped, therefore, that all clubs will come forward and cooperate in this movement, so that it may be as universal as possible, and insure the adoption of one code of rules, and one ball to govern the game of tennis throughout the whole of the United States. Clubs wishing to cooperate and be represented at the convention will please notify the representatives of either of the three organizing clubs, whose addresses are given below, and regular forms of application, together with further particulars will be forwarded to them.

The notice was signed by Clarence M. Clark, Chairman of the Philadelphia Committee, from Germantown, Pennsylvania, E. H. Outerbridge, of New York, secretary of the Staten Island Club, and James Dwight, of Boston, representative to the Beacon Park Athletic Association.

On May 21, 1881, the representatives from various clubs met in a New York hotel to standardize rules, the heights of nets, size of rackets, weight of balls, and other details. The U.S. National Lawn Tennis Association (later just USLTA) was off to a good start; that August and September saw the first official National Men's Singles Championships on the grass of the Newport casino. (A locale that lasted until 1914, when the tournament moved on permanently to Forest Hills.)

The U.S. Lawn Tennis Association quickly became the force behind American tennis and how it was to be played. The USLTA created the idea of umpires and referees, and of official rankings. (In 1885, there were only ten men skilled enough to be ranked.) Interestingly most of the rules were well established by 1895; since then, only minor changes have been made.

During these decades the general public didn't get much opportunity to play, for tennis remained the preserve of America's moneyed. It was logical that the upper social strata could—and would—insist on pure amateurism. The competitors were financially well endowed through their family or professions, and the reward for winning was not cash but enormous silver trophies. In 1900, for instance, Dwight F. Davis, a St. Louis millionaire–tennis player, put up a silver bowl worth $700 (much at the time), and thereby launched the first Davis Cup Matches.

The U.S.L.T.A. encouraged the awarding of cups at an early stage in the game's development. *Photo by Max Peter Haas.*

Each year, however, women made greater inroads, with more courts being occupied by lady competitors in long dresses and short-sleeved white blouses, some with curious men's ties. In 1887, the Philadelphia Cricket Club held the first National Women's Title matches. From 1912 onward, Mary K. Browne, a champion golfer, also swung a tennis racket. Photos survive that show the determined faces of these first American women players. One example was Hazel Hotchkiss Wightman, who donated a cup herself. Women from many countries battled it out at Wimbledon, the white shoes and long white stockings racing across the famous close-cropped lawns.

At the National Tennis Hall of Fame, in Newport, Rhode Island, there still stands a huge, sturdy shipping box that dates back to 1920; such trunklike contraptions transported rackets from and to faraway places like "Australasia." (Then the term combined Australia and New Zealand.) Indeed, British and American champions were now facing a crop of Australians. Suzanne Lenglen, a superbly talented Frenchwoman, made a name for herself during the twenties, which was the time, too, of France's hard-playing "Four Musketeers," Jean Borotra, René Lacoste, Henri Cochet, and Jacques Brugnon.

Since 1920, America's William (Big Bill) Tilden, 2nd, had dazzled the world by winning the men's singles at Wimbledon. Tilden, a graceful six-footer had taken up tennis when he was a small boy. He perfected his strokes and strategy to such a degree that he won most matches between 1920 and 1930. René Lacoste, his frequent adversary, once described Tilden in action:

> Seemingly, in two steps Tilden covers the whole of the court; without any effort he executes the most various and extraordinary strokes. He seems capable of returning any shot, if he likes to put the ball out of reach of his opponent when he thinks the moment has come to do so. Sometimes he gives the ball prodigious velocity, sometimes he caresses it and guides it to a corner of the court whither nobody but himself would have thought of directing it.

Tilden, the "autocrat of the courts" remained U.S. singles champion for seven years and won the Davis Cup numerous times. He may have been the greatest player ever produced by the United States.

It is intriguing to note, from the vantage point of the profit-conscious present, that Bill Tilden stuck to his amateur guns as long as he could. The code was so strict that Tilden, a former actor and a capable writer, got into hot water merely because he wrote tennis articles for money.

During the late twenties and early thirties, other great names, such as Helen Wills Moody, Bill Johnston, George Lott, and Pancho Segura, began to appear in the headlines. Few players had ambitions to earn a great deal from the sport; they were mostly interested in recouping their travel and living expenses and garnering victories for their country. "It was on the

U.S. Wightman Cup team—1924. *Photo courtesy United States Lawn Tennis Association.*

whole a carefree life," recalls one player, who was "living from day to day, sometimes richly, the next moment traveling in trains with eight people in the compartment." Some male tournament champions contented themselves with the $10-per-diems and the many female admirers, the good hotels at the French Riviera, the glamour of Monte Carlo, and free trips to San Francisco and Los Angeles. A few competitors took money in secret for endorsements and nonexistent expenses.

Professional tennis began in 1926 with the exhibition matches of Harvey Snowgrass, Vincent Richards, Bruce Barnes and others whose careers have been forgotten. The earnings were small by comparison with today's and so were the audiences. Tennis was still relatively unimportant as a university sport; Gardnar Mulloy remembers that in 1931 Florida's colleges had "no courts, no teams, no scholarships, no campus games." Indoor courts were scarce around the country. Good rackets could be bought for fifteen dollars. Golf took precedence at the country clubs; tennis clubs sought members. It was true that tennis had become more attractive; the ladies were at last getting out of their white dresses and into shorts sans stockings; male athletes bared their bronzed knees. All the same, prestigious tournament finals at the Greenbrier, in West Virginia, fetched only two hundred spectators.

In 1930, Tilden turned professional, and things changed with real promotion of pro tennis. After some years as a successful amateur, California's Ellsworth Vines succumbed to the lure of the dollar. Bobby Riggs and Don Budge soon got into the act. After World War II, Jack Kramer, a former champion, and a first-rate tennis technician, signed up many international names for a pro "Circus." Kramer, a good organizer, saw to it that his celebrity players made money. The amateurs went on playing at Wimbledon and elsewhere, but eventually Kramer had drawn many of the big names into his camp. "Open tennis" experienced some last-ditch resistance, until in 1968, when the last bastions fell. Pros and amateurs were now allowed to mingle and compete against one another. At the same time, such powerfully financed pro promotions as World Championship Tennis (WCT) began to flourish. Television brought prosperity to women players, who started their own professional troupes touring the land, playing for enormous sums put up by cigarette companies and other sponsors. Talented players, such as Billie Jean King (who during the fifties still depended on benevolent friends and fans to send her to competitions), signed mind-boggling contracts during the mid-seventies with yearly earnings that dwarfed those of an IBM or a General Motors president.

While tennis has a bright future for the pro ranks and for industry, the average adult and child also stands an ever-increasing chance to play and compete. Americans no longer need wealth and pedigrees to become tennis players, and some of them will make competitive history in the future.

# Selected Bibliography

Addie, Pauline Betz, *Tennis for Everyone,* Washington, D. C.: Acropolis.

BP Yearbook, *World of Tennis, Yearly,* London: Queen Anne Press.

Danzig, Allison, and Peter Schwed, editors, *The Fireside Book of Tennis,* New York: Simon and Schuster.

Fadiman, Edwin, Jr., *The Professional,* New York: David McKay.

Grimsley, Will, *Tennis, Its History, People and Events,* Englewood Cliffs, New Jersey: Prentice-Hall.

Metzler, Paul, *Tennis Styles and Stylists,* New York: Macmillan.

Mottram, Tony, *Play Better Tennis,* New York: Ace Books.

Murphy, Chet, *Advanced Tennis,* Dubuque, Iowa: Brown Publishers.

Richards, Gilbert, *Tennis for Travelers,* Cincinnati: Gilbert Richards.

Riessen, Marty, and Richard Evans, *Match Point,* Englewood Cliffs, New Jersey: Prentice-Hall.

Scharff, Robert, *The Quick and Easy Guide to Tennis,* New York: Collier.

Scott, Eugene *Tennis: Game of Motion,* New York: Rutledge/Crown.

*Sports Illustrated Book of Tennis,* Philadelphia: Lippincott.

Talbert, Bill, *Weekend Tennis,* Garden City, New York: Doubleday.

Talbert, William F., and Bruce S. Old, *The Game of Doubles in Tennis,* Philadelphia: Lippincott.

Trengove, Alan, ed., *The Art of Tennis,* London: Hodder & Stoughton.

*USLTA, Official Encyclopedia of Tennis,* New York: Harper & Row.

Warren, Wind, ed., *The Realm of Sport,* New York: Simon and Schuster.

World Tennis Magazine and Cornel Lumiere, *The Book of Tennis—How to Play the Game,* New York: Grosset & Dunlap.

Zwieg, John, *Courtside Companion,* San Francisco: Chronicle.

## TENNIS PUBLICATIONS

*Tennis Magazine,* 297 Westport Ave., Norwalk, Conn. 06856

*World Tennis,* 8100 Westglen, Houston, Texas 77042

*Tennis West,* P. O. Box 5048, Santa Monica, Calif. 90405

*Tennis Industry,* 14961 N. E. 6th Avenue, North Miami, Florida 33161

# Tennis Glossary

ACE—A perfect service that the receiver fails to touch.

AD-IN, AD-OUT—Game-scoring terms for "advantage" to the server and advantage to receiver.

APPROACH SHOT—A shot allowing the player to advance toward the net.

BACKHAND—Any stroke taken to the left side of the player. (Reverse for left-hander.)

BACKSWING—That part of the stroke taken in preparation before the ball is struck. The rest of the stroke usually includes a "follow-through."

CENTER SERVICE LINE—The line dividing the service court into halves and separating the right and left service courts.

CHANGE-OF-PACE—Shots made with varying power and speed.

CHOP—A downward angled stroke that carries a great deal of backspin.

CHOKING—Psychological inhibition that prevents a player from swinging properly.

CONTINENTAL GRIP—A grip that permits both forehand and backhand playing.

CROSS-COURT SHOT—A stroke hit across to the opposite side of the court. A diagonal shot.

DEUCE—The moment when both players reach 40/40—i.e., the same number of points. To win the game, one player must get two points in a row.

DOWN-THE-LINE—A stroke hit down the sideline from the same originating side.

DINK—A soft delivery just across the net, often at wide angles.

DROP SHOT—A stroke hit with backspin that barely clears the net and has limited forward motion following the bounce.

DROP VOLLEY—A shot delivered without letting the ball bounce. A drop volley lands short on the other side of the net.

DRIVE—A shot hit after the bounce with a full motion.

FAULT—A service that does not land in the proper court. A double fault means a second unsuccessful service and a point to the receiver.

FOOT FAULT—A loss of point due to server's toe or foot crossing the base line before the ball hits racket.

FOREHAND—Any stroke taken to the right side of the player (reverse for left-hander).

GAME—The fourth point won by a player, unless there is a deuce, whereupon the player must score two consecutive points.

GRAND SLAM—The feat of winning the singles championships of Australia, France, and Wimbledon in the same year.

GROUND STROKE—A ball hit after it has bounced.

HALF VOLLEY—A stroke used in hitting a ball almost immediately after the bounce.

HEAD—The frame and strings of the racket.

LET—A service that hits the net but falls into the proper court, or a point that is replayed.

LOB—A ball propelled high into the air and over the opponent's head.

LOVE—A term used in game-scoring to mean zero or nothing.

MATCH POINT—The point that, if won by the player who is ahead, wins the match. A final point.

NET PLAY—Rushing the net and playing at the net.

PASSING SHOT—A ball that passes the net man.

PLACEMENT—A shot that cannot be returned by the opposing player.

POACHING—When a doubles player infringes on partner's territory.

PSYCH—Breaking down an opponent psychologically.

PUT AWAY—A shot hit so perfectly that no return can be made.

RALLY—A long series of ball exchanges in which both players are able to keep the ball in play. A "rally" should not be confused with a "volley."

RECEIVER—The player who receives the service. The sequence changes after each game.

SERVER—The player who serves.

SERVICE—The stroke that puts the ball into play.

SET—A series of six games won by a player. It may be more games, but they must be won by a margin of two.

SET POINT—One point, which, if won by the player who is ahead, wins the set.

SLICE—A ground stroke or volley hit on a near-horizontal plane.

SMASH—An overhead stroke, the usual answer to the lob. Also called an "overhead."

TOPSPIN—A ball rotating on a vertical plane from backward to forward.

VOLLEY—Hitting a ball before it has touched the ground.

# Index